Penguin Education
Penguin Science of Behaviour
General Editor: B. M. Foss

Developmental Psychology
Editor: B. M. Foss

Psychometric Assessment of the
Individual Child
R. Douglass Savage

Psychometric Assessment of the Individual Child

R. Douglass Savage

Penguin Books

Penguin Books Ltd, Harmondsworth,
Middlesex, England
Penguin Books Inc., 7110 Ambassador Road,
Baltimore, Md 21207, U.S.A.
Penguin Books Australia Ltd, Ringwood,
Victoria, Australia

First published 1968
Reprinted 1969
Copyright © R. Douglass Savage, 1968

Made and printed in Great Britain by
Hazell Watson & Viney Ltd,
Aylesbury, Bucks
Set in Linotype Plantin

To Karen, Lois and Inge,
with the hope that the merging of scientific
methodology and sympathetic understanding
may help children everywhere fulfil their
individual potential

Penguin Science of Behaviour

This book is one of the first in an ambitious project, the *Penguin Science of Behaviour*, which will cover a very wide range of psychological inquiry. Many of the short 'unit' texts will be on central teaching topics, while others will deal with present theoretical and empirical work which the Editors consider to be important new contributions to psychology. We have kept in mind both the teaching divisions of psychology and also the needs of psychologists at work. For readers working with children, for example, some of the units in the field of Developmental Psychology will deal with techniques in testing children, other units will deal with work on cognitive growth. For academic psychologists, there will be units in well-established areas such as Learning and Perception, but also units which do not fall neatly under any one heading, or which are thought of as 'applied', but which nevertheless are highly relevant to psychology as a whole.

The project is published in short units for two main reasons. Firstly, a large range of short texts at inexpensive prices gives the teacher a flexibility in planning his course and recommending texts for it. Secondly, the pace at which important new work is published requires the project to be adaptable. Our plan allows a unit to be revised or a fresh unit to be added with maximum speed and minimal cost to the reader.

Above all, for students, the different viewpoints of many authors, sometimes overlapping, sometimes in contradiction, and the range of topics Editors have selected will reveal the complexity and diversity which exist beyond the necessarily conventional headings of an introductory course.

B.M.F.

Contents

Editorial Foreword

Child psychology began at the end of the last century, and there have been several lines of development. Children are studied for comparative purposes, so that their thinking can be compared with that of adults for instance; on the other hand, the psychological study of almost any process (learning, perceiving, etc.) includes a developmental aspect, and these processes are therefore all studied in children, and also in the aged. This developmental approach is now receiving a great deal of attention, and in the last decade there has been a great increase in the study of infant behaviour. The rationale is that processes are more likely to be understood if their beginnings have been investigated. Much of this work is relatively unbiassed theoretically, although psychologists do still develop new and modify old theories of child development.

However, children have been and are now studied for their own sake. This is especially true when decisions have to be taken about their education or their mental health. The testing movement in psychology has very much depended on educational and clinical psychologists working with children, but the tests they have produced may be used by many kinds of psychologist. The first unit text in Developmental Psychology is about the very special techniques and skills involved in testing individual children.

The author, Dr Savage, is highly experienced in this field. He is critical of many of the tests which are available, and rightly so. His balanced account will be of use to psychology undergraduates as well as professional psychologists.

B.M.F.

Acknowledgements

I am indebted to my educational, medical, psychological, speech and social worker colleagues and students for the valuable suggestions they have given me on the problems of communicating psychometric information to other disciplines.

In particular, I acknowledge the interest of Professor Donald Court of the Child Health Department and Mrs Mary Harris, Head of the Speech and Speech Pathology Department, both at the University of Newcastle upon Tyne. The valuable comments on the manuscript of Mr David Johnston, headmaster and psychologist, of the Percy Hedley Spastic School, Forest Hall, Newcastle upon Tyne, were also greatly appreciated.

I am also grateful to Professor Brian Foss, the General Editor of the Penguin Science of Behaviour series, for his interest, encouragement and assistance.

Finally, I would like to thank Miss Pauline Bowey for withstanding the difficulties of typing this manuscript.

R.D.S.

1 Introduction

The aim of this book is to bring to the attention of student and practising psychologists, and also to medical, educational and social science workers, some of the traditional and more recent developments in psychometric techniques for assessing the individual child. Increasingly, the results of such assessments are being transmitted from discipline to discipline in the interests of the child. Care must be taken that those receiving psychometric assessment reports fully understand the interpretation of these data, their *potential* and their *limitations*. The chain – from the psychologist's dictated report, via the psychiatrist, paediatrician, family doctor, teacher, social worker, child care officer, committee or individual, to the recommendations for treatment or advice to parents and housemothers – is a long one: the dangers of misinterpretation and catastrophy for the individual child resulting from confusion at any stage must not be lightly brushed aside. I hope this book will help reduce such dangers. I wish to present (and hope I have achieved) a readable, yet scientifically sound, description of the psychometric measurement techniques commonly or, at least, increasingly used in assessing the individual child by psychologists in clinical and educational practice.

The book has chapters covering the assessment of intellectual, educational, personality and motor-perceptual characteristics and is completed by examples of the comprehensive assessment undertaken on some typical clinical–educational problem children. The aim has been to be up to date, yet not too technical, accurate, but not too precise, comprehensive without being too lengthy, to stress the scientific precision and methodology necessary to develop measurement techniques for child behaviour, and at the same time to be aware of their present limitations.

Much has been written, and even more said, about the role of the applied psychologist. For many reasons, the educational and clinical psychologist – the psychologist most associated with children – has adopted a multitude of roles. I feel, however, that any effort to examine the contribution which applied psychology might bring to the study, understanding and aid of 'the child' must first look at the origins of applied psychology itself.

The distinctive contribution which psychology can make to applied problems would appear to me to be derived from academic training in psychology. The development of standardized, reliable and, above all, valid measures of cognitive and personality characteristics, and the increase in understanding of perception and learning come from the basic knowledge in what might be regarded as the 'arena of academic psychology'. The most significant result of training in psychology, however, appears to be the attitude that scientific methodology can and, indeed, must be applied to the investigation of *human behaviour*, whether it be normal or abnormal, child or adult. This attitude epitomizes recent developments and teaching in academic psychology. Why all this as a universal prerequisite to training in applied psychology, if it is not to be used there? Far too often we see applied psychologists adopting a well-meaning, but misguided role, oblivious to the value of their three or four years' undergraduate training and often even their other two or three years' postgraduate training, acting much too often like well-meaning laymen and not appreciating the contribution that their subject might make to the problems presented in the clinic.

I am not advocating here that applied psychology should be dynamic and follow psychoanalytic dynamically oriented personality theory and practice, or that it should be atomistic and behavioural in its approach to human problems. I am simply arguing for a sound, rigorous and scientific approach to problems of human behaviour by the psychologist, as well as a humane role. I am not suggesting that psychologists should just diagnose, treat, or carry out research. They may and indeed should do one or all three of these things. The crucial point is that they should approach their work with psychological knowledge and techniques; for example, with well-standardized, reliable and valid tests for diagnoses, sound experimentally based techniques for treatment, and a good knowledge of the research literature and problems in the area which they are investigating. Clinical intuition and a well-meaning attitude have an important part to play in the psychologist's repertoire, but these are by no means the prerogative of the psychologist. The doctor, the social worker and the educationist have them, but they also bring their own training and techniques to the aid of the child. The psychologist must do the same to justify his existence (Savage, 1968).

In this book I do not intend to discuss the treatment and research areas of psychological investigation of the individual child, but to present some of the assessment techniques related to the question of sorting out the complex issues of diagnosis. The advent of psychometric techniques has been revolutionary in terms of our understanding of the personality and cognitive factors in human development and can make a significant contribution to helping the individual child.

The first major problem facing any clinician is to know how the child relates to others. Experience has taught us that as individuals our ability to assess personality or intelligence on the basis of physical features, social background, 'clinical intuition' and the like can be far from satisfactory. This has led to the development of what have become known as standardized, psychometric measures. The cognitive or intellectual field led in this respect. The pioneer work of Binet was followed by more and more refined techniques and newer versions of the Stanford–Binet Intelligence Test in 1937 and 1960. Another test of major importance to the investigation of children's cognitive behaviour is the Wechsler Intelligence Scale for Children. This test was developed in 1949 and is available for the age range five to fifteen. It has many advantages over the Binet in that it breaks intelligence down into many sub-categories and provides normative data on all sub-scale areas, not just giving a general I.Q. figure. Similar techniques are now being developed in relation to the measurement of personality in the children's area. I can mention the Cattell scales which are now available to cover no less than thirteen personality characteristics from six years upwards, and the Eysenck Personality Inventory with more limited questionnaire assessment of neuroticism and extraversion from seven years of age. These measures will be dealt with in detail in the later chapters.

The main purpose of the present section is to introduce an understanding of the basis upon which psychometric measures stand. They develop from extremely complicated mathematical techniques which cannot be profitably discussed here (Nunnally, 1967). It is fortunate, however, that behaviour characteristics tend to distribute in the form of a normal curve. This fact, combined with the development of statistical psychometric procedures over the last sixty years or so, has made possible the more exact measurement of individual differences.

The problem is to be able to assess the child on a certain characteristic in terms of some quantitative variable to give him a score – for example, intelligence 100, neuroticism 15, extroversion 20. Having got these figures, one must have a frame of reference within which to interpret them and here the characteristics of the normal curve and the statistical procedures related to this have been of immense value. It is now possible to measure many human characteristics and to calculate the way in which each characteristic distributes in the population. This *standardization* of a test is done by widespread, usually random sampling of children representing various age levels and both sexes. A single psychometric measure may require the investigation of several thousand children and extensive statistical analysis of the data. The *mean* and the *standard deviation* (S.D.) or distribution of the characteristic must be found. A child can then be positioned in relation to other children along certain dimensions such as intelligence, aggression, emotional stability, motor ability and social maturity. Consequently, a profile on the 'whole child' may be mapped. In order to develop adequate measures of each characteristic, one must look at specific aspects of the child. This does not in any way mean that the child is not regarded as a 'whole', but merely that in order to understand this whole, its component parts must be measured.

The tests developed must, moreover, be *reliable* as well as widely standardized. By reliable, we mean that whenever individuals are measured on this apparatus their scores will be consistent. This, in fact, is done by calculating the split half correlation of items or the correlation coefficient between test and retest scores over various intervals of time on the same individuals. Such a procedure indicates that the measures used, for example the Wechsler Intelligence Scale for Children or the Cattell Personality Scales, are consistent in measuring the same thing. It does not tell us, however, whether they are measuring what we want them to measure. This raises one of the most difficult problems in applied psychology, the problem of *validity*. There are four main categories or types of validity used in constructing tests. The first two of these are criterion-oriented validation procedures. That is to say, the investigator is primarily interested in some criterion which he wishes to predict with this test. For example, he may wish to develop a test for measuring neurosis. In this case, he may relate the psychiatrist's assessment of neurotic behaviour to the measurement obtained from the psychometric procedure. If the criterion is obtained some time *after* the test is given, he is studying *predictive validity*: for example, when an I.Q.

test is given and related to subsequent success in 'O' level examinations. If the test score and the criterion score are determined at essentially the same time, he is measuring *concurrent validity*. This may happen when a new measure of educational attainment is compared with teacher estimates collected at the same time.

Content validity, another technique used in developing psychometric measures, is established by a somewhat different method. In this case, it is necessary to know whether the items used, for example intelligence test items, are a genuine sample of intellectual questions. In building up an intelligence test, items which are believed to be of an intellectual nature are selected from a large number of possible items. The content validity of each item is measured by first correlating each item with the total score on the test. This method is applicable to the development of all psychometric measures.

The fourth, and probably the most complicated method of validating a psychometric measure is *construct validation*. In this case, the test is used to assess some quality which may not be perfectly defined or understood. We ask ourselves what constructs or dimensions of the child account for individual differences in performances on the test or on certain tasks. Much current research on tests of personality involves construct validation. Cattell found he was able to organize the measurement of personality of children eight to twelve years old in terms of fourteen factors or characteristics. It must be used whenever any criterion or universe of content is not accepted as entirely adequate (or is not available) to define the quality to be measured, for example when looking for new methods of describing and analysing the whole child.

In subsequent chapters, the methodology of constructing psychometric tests will no doubt be clarified by the descriptions and discussion of measures which have been undertaken. One need not feel apprehensive if terms like construct validation are somewhat difficult to grasp, as many professional psychologists after six years' training have similar problems. The main purpose of this book is to outline and discuss the psychometric measures, *not* their methods of construction. As a limited number of statistical concepts, however, are necessarily introduced in the text, a brief glossary of these terms is provided in the Appendix, page 100. Details of the methods can be found in Maxwell (1958), Meehl (1954), McNemar (1963) and Nunnally (1967).

Finally, I wish to stress that psychometric techniques have important implications and value for the normal individual child, as well as for the clinical – educational problem child.

2 The Measurement of Intellect

Intellectual, cognitive or mental ability was one of the first human behavioural characteristics to come under the canopy of scientific measurement. It defined the content of the first and now most well known of psychometric measures – intelligence tests. Although these are the most widely used psychometric measures, they are still far from being fully understood and often misused – especially in the assessment of the individual child.

The great impetus for the measurement of intelligence came in the early twentieth century when the French Minister of Public Instruction appointed a commission to study the education of subnormal children in the Paris area, and Binet and Simon collaborated to develop their first (1905) scale of thirty intellectual problems arranged in order of difficulty. This scale was revised in 1908 and 1911 and the concept of *mental age* introduced. Later, in 1916, the popular English Language Stanford–Binet Scales were developed by Terman and his colleagues, and revised in 1937 and 1960 to present the concept of the Intelligence Quotient (I.Q.) (Terman and Merrill, 1960).

There have been many developments of individual and group psychometric measures of intelligence since the early work of Wundt, Galton, Cattell, Binet and Terman. However, in the clinical–educational assessment of cognitive functioning in the individual child, *two* measures are of outstanding importance and are now in widespread use – the 1960 forms L–M of the Stanford–Binet and the Wechsler Intelligence Scale for Children (Wechsler, 1949). This chapter will devote most of its attention to these two tests and also discuss a major British contribution to the area of cognitive measurement – Raven's Coloured Progressive Matrices (Raven, 1947–53). As stated in the introduction, I will deal primarily with intellectual measurement of the age range five to fifteen, so I will not discuss such pre-school intelligence scales as the Griffiths and the Minnesota pre-school measures.

First, however, a few words about the major concepts and statistics behind intelligence testing (Guilford, 1967; Nunnally, 1967). What is I.Q.? How can we compare children on this characteristic? The methodology behind the development of intelligence tests is the basis of human behavioural measurement and became possible only because of the advances in mathematical statistics seen in the writings of Karl Pearson and Fisher. The twin development of normal curve statistics and the behavioural findings of Galton and others that many human characteristics were normally distributed led to the innovation of more exact 'psychometric' measures of human characteristics and our ability to assess the individual.

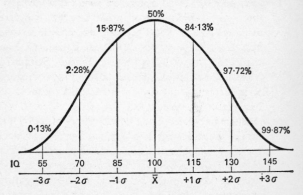

Figure 1 Intelligence quotient distribution – the normal curve

If test results are normally distributed, as intelligence scores are, the average person will have an I.Q. score of 100. Fifty per cent of the population will be above and 50 per cent below that score. What is more important, is that intelligence also spreads throughout the population in a certain way. The normal curve has three standard deviations each side of it covering 99·98 per cent of the population and can be divided into percentile points so that the number of persons expected to obtain a certain score can be estimated according to the mathematical properties of the normal curve. Thus 84·13 per cent of the population on an intelligence test with a mean of 100 and standard deviation 15 would score 115 or less, a score of 130 or above would be obtained by only 2·28 per cent of the population. On the lower side only 2·28 per cent would score less than 70 and so on.

An I.Q. is therefore a measure which places a child in relation to other children of the same age. If the test is so constructed that the means and standard deviations are the same for all age groups, a child's score at one age level can be easily compared with his score at an earlier or eventually later age, and results from children of different age groups can be compared.

In assessing the individual child in the clinic, we use principally the Stanford–Binet, the Wechsler Intelligence Scale for Children and the Raven's Matrices intellectual measures. Each has its strengths and weaknesses, uses and abuses, so I will now outline each of these tests and discuss their application.

Stanford–Binet Intelligence Scale (Terman and Merrill, 1960)

Originally developed in 1916 by Terman at Stanford University from the earlier test introduced by Binet in 1905, the Stanford–Binet was most recently revised in 1960. This form of the test extends from the age of two years to the adult level, but it is used most commonly with children. Most of the items are oral, although some require the subject to read, write, draw, or carry out simple manipulative tasks.

The materials needed for administering the Stanford–Binet include a box of standard toy objects for use with younger children, a set of printed cards, a record booklet for recording responses (or an abbreviated record form), and a test manual. The tasks to be performed by the subject in the various Stanford–Binet tests run the gamut from simple manipulation to abstract reasoning. The following description is intended only to illustrate the wide variety of content covered by these scales and should not be construed as a complete listing of item types.

A few tests at the earliest age levels involve the manipulation of objects and a certain amount of eye–hand coordination. Among them may be mentioned the simple formboard, in which the three pieces must be inserted into the appropriate recesses, as well as tests involving block building, stringing beads, and drawing tests in which the child copies a circle, a square, or a diamond. Tests of perceptual discrimination occur at the lower age levels, examples including comparison of the lengths of sticks and matching geometric forms. A relatively large number of items at the lower levels involve the observation and identification of common objects, such as pointing to parts of the body in a large picture of a doll. Some tests require the subject to name objects, or pictures of objects, whilst others call for the completion of pictures, or the identification of the missing parts. Several questions ask the subject to state the similarities or differences between certain sets of objects named by the examiner.

Practical judgement or common sense is also measured by a series of 'comprehension' questions in which the child is asked what he should do when meeting certain everyday life situations. In other similar tests at these and higher year levels, the subject is required to explain why certain practices are commonly followed or certain objects are employed in daily living. A number of tests calling for the interpretation of pictorially or verbally presented situations, or the detection of absurdities in either pictures or brief stories, also seem to fall into this category. Memory tests are found throughout the scale and utilize a wide variety of materials. The subject is required to recall or recognize objects, pictures, geometric designs, bead patterns, digits, sentences, and the content of passages.

Spatial orientation questions, which include maze-tracing, paper-folding, paper-cutting, rearrangements of geometric figures, and directional orientation, occur at widely scattered levels. Numerical tests range from rudimentary quantitative concepts, counting, and the simple arithmetic problems encountered in elementary school, to more complex arithmetic reasoning problems involving novel solutions and the inductive formulation of rules.

The most numerous type of item in the Stanford–Binet is that employing verbal content, such well-known tests as vocabulary, analogies, sentence completion, disarranged sentences, defining abstract terms, and interpreting proverbs being included.

Like most intelligence tests designed for clinical use, the Stanford–Binet is an individual test. It can be administered to only one subject at a time and requires a trained examiner. In such a situation it is possible for the clinician to gain rapport with the child and to observe the subject's work methods, attitudes, and problem-solving techniques, as well as the finished product. Interpersonal reactions, emotional responses, and other incidental behaviour can likewise be noted.

The Stanford–Binet yields a single score expressed as a deviation I.Q. with a mean of 100 and an S.D. of 16. In addition, it is claimed that one of the chief advantages of the Stanford–Binet is derived from the mass of interpretive data and extensive clinical experience that have been accumulated regarding this test. For many clinicians, educators, and others concerned with the evaluation of general ability level, the Stanford–Binet I.Q. has become almost synonymous with intelligence. Much has been learned on the sort of behaviour expected from a child with an I.Q. of 50 or 80 or 120 from this test.

In interpreting the I.Q., it should be borne in mind that the Stanford–Binet is primarily a measure of scholastic aptitude and heavily loaded with verbal functions, especially at the upper levels. Individuals with a language handicap, as well as those whose strongest abilities lie along non-verbal lines will thus score relatively low on such a test. Similarly, there are undoubtedly a number of fields in which scholastic aptitude and verbal comprehension are not of primary importance. Obviously to apply any test to situations for which it is inappropriate will only reduce its effectiveness. Because of the common identification of Stanford–Binet I.Q. with the very concept of intelligence, there has been a tendency to expect too much from this one test.

Short form

In concluding this description of the Stanford–Binet mention should be made of the abbreviated scale. Four tests in each year level were selected on this basis of validity and representativeness to constitute a short scale for use when time does not permit the administration of the entire scale. Comparisons between full-scale and abbreviated-scale I.Q.s on a variety of groups show a close correspondence between the two. The mean I.Q., however, tends to run slightly lower on the short scale, a discrepancy that is brought out even more vividly when individual cases are considered. Both forms, however, give only a simple classification score, a major limitation of the test.

The Coloured Progressive Matrices (Raven, 1947–53)

John Raven developed the original Progressive Matrices in 1938, a measure consisting of sixty perceptually presented tests. Each test consists of a design or 'matrix' from which part has been removed. The testee has to examine the matrix and decide which of six pieces given below is the right one to complete the matrix. Twelve items make up a set and there are five sets, lettered A to E. The first problem in a set is intended to be self-evident, and it is succeeded by twelve problems of increasingly difficulty.

The themes employed were (A) continuous patterns, (B) analogies between pairs of figures, (C) progressive alterations of patterns, (D) permutations of figures, and (E) resolution of figures into constituent parts.

For children from three to eight years of age and for the mentally defective, sets A and B were arranged as coloured patterns in book and cardboard form. For normal subjects over the age of eight years, the matrices in sets A, B, C, D, and E were drawn in black and white and mounted. The number of problems correctly solved represented the subject's total score and the test may be given by self-administration or group testing. Verbal instructions can be reduced to a minimum.

In 1947, the Coloured Progressive Matrices sets A, Ab and B were constructed for children between five to eleven years of age. To attract and hold the attention of young children, each problem was printed on a brightly coloured background. This makes the nature of the problem to be solved more obvious without in any way contributing to its solution. The order of the problems in each set provides the standard training in the method of working and the three sets together are arranged to cover all the perceptual reasoning processes of which children under twelve years of age are usually capable. If the test is suitably presented, it is necessary only to show a person what to do, to let him work through the problems in the standard order and to learn to solve them from his own experience. The test can be presented in the form of boards and movable pieces, or as illustrations printed in a book, without the intellectual processes required for success being essentially altered. In either form the problems to be solved can be demonstrated quite satisfactorily with virtually no verbal instructions.

Raven (1947), described the test as 'constructed to give, for children of five to eleven years of age, a wider dispersion of scores, to reduce the frequency of chance solutions and to make the test more suitable for use with persons who are for any reason mentally subnormal or impaired.' He claimed a test–retest reliability of 0·65 for children under seven, by age nine, a test–retest reliability of 0·80, and over the whole range for which the test was constructed a test–retest reliability of 0·9. The test has been widely used with mentally defective, as well as normal children.

Special studies of the Progressive Matrices (Burke, 1966) have been published for many groups: the deaf, the cerebral palsied, mental defectives, adult psychiatric patients, child guidance clinical patients, army recruits, university or professional students and apprentices. One may ask, however, what do the tests actually measure? Opinion begins with statements by the author: 'By itself it is not a test of "General Intelligence".' Rather he has spoken of it as a 'means of estimating a person's innate eductive ability', as designed to measure 'accuracy of eduction', as a 'test of a person's present capacity to form comparisons, reason by analogy, and develop a logical method of thinking regardless of previously acquired information.' On the other hand, Raven offered a definition of intellectual ability as the 'ability to reason by analogy from awareness of relations between experienced characters'.

Spearman considered Raven's Progressive Matrices a test for measuring *g* or eduction, in fact, perhaps the best of all non-verbal tests of *g*. This has been the general English opinion, supported by such workers as Philip Vernon, Professor of Educational Psychology, University of Calgary, Alberta.

The C.P.M. (Coloured Progressive Matrices) (Raven, 1947) cannot be considered a substitute for the Stanford–Binet or the Wechsler tests, but the correlations of these tests with the C.P.M. with children seem as high as the correlations reported for these tests with each other in similar populations, between 0·6 and 0·9. In view of its ease of administration and the time required, the C.P.M. seems worthy of further study by item analyses, cross-validation studies, and by collecting normative data for special groups. It is a promising test widely used in educational and clinical practice in Great Britain, but still requiring further research. Like the Stanford–Binet, however, it gives only a single I.Q. score, this time non-verbal, but there is a complementary Crichton Vocabulary Scale for this test.

The Wechsler Intelligence Scale for Children (Wechsler, 1949)

The Wechsler Intelligence Scale for Children (W.I.S.C.) is undoubtedly the most widely used clinical intelligence measure. It is an extremely versatile, efficient and pleasant tool to work with, usually enjoyed by child and examiner alike.

The W.I.S.C. was prepared in 1949 as a downward extension of the Wechsler–Bellevue Intelligence Scale, an adult measure developed in 1944. It consists of twelve subtests of which two are used as alternatives or supplementary tests where time permits. The subtests are grouped into a verbal and a performance scale, so that verbal I.Q., performance I.Q. and full scale I.Q. can be derived. In addition, the discrepancy between verbal and performance I.Q. and subtest score differences can be assessed, some of which have been found to have important clinical implications. The W.I.S.C. scales are set out below.

Full scale

Verbal scales		*Performance scales*	
1	General information	6	Picture completion
2	General comprehension	7	Picture arrangement
3	Arithmetic	8	Block design
4	Similarities	9	Object assembly
5	Vocabulary	10	Coding
(11)	Digit span	(12)	Mazes

The tests listed as alternatives, Digit span (11) and

Mazes (12), were those giving the lowest correlations with the rest of the scale.

Norms and scoring procedures

The treatment of scores on the W.I.S.C. follows a standard procedure (Wechsler, 1949); raw scores on each subtest are first changed into normalized standard scores within the subject's own age group. Tables of such scaled scores are provided for every four-month interval between the ages of five and fifteen years. Each subtest scaled score is expressed in terms of a distribution with a mean of 10 and an S.D. of 3 points. The verbal (5), performance (5) and full scale I.Q.s (10) subscales are combined and converted into I.Q. measures with a mean of 100 and an S.D. of 15.

The standardization sample of an American population for the W.I.S.C. was thorough and representative, including 100 boys and 100 girls at each age from five through fifteen years, giving a total of 2200 cases. All subjects were obtained from schools with the exception of fifty-five mental defectives, who were tested in institutions for the feebleminded. Testing was carried out in eighty-five communities located in all states, as well as in three institutions for mental defectives. The distribution of subjects conformed closely to the 1940 U.S. census for the country at large, in terms of geographical area, urban–rural proportion, and parental occupation. In many respects, the W.I.S.C. standardization sample is almost certainly more representative of a country at large than any other sample employed in standardizing individual tests.

The W.I.S.C. is a highly reliable test in which correlation coefficients are reported between each pair of subtests, as well as for verbal, performance, and full scale scores. These reliabilities were computed separately within the 7½-, 10½-, and 13½-year sample, each age group consisting of 200 cases. The full scale I.Q. reliability coefficients for the three age levels were 0.92, 0.95, and 0.94 respectively, for the verbal scale were 0.88, 0.96, and 0·96, and for the performance scale 0·86, 0·89, and 0·90.

The subtest reliabilities are slightly less, ranging from the 0·50s to the 0·90s. It might be added that most of the subtests had lower reliability coefficients in the youngest age group than in the other two groups. The test manual rightly cautions the users of this scale against interpreting differences between subtest scores without due reference to the reliability coefficients of the particular subtests, a caution much too often disregarded by practising clinicians. A four-year follow-up indicated that W.I.S.C. I.Q.s are about as stable as Stanford–Binet I.Q.s over such an interval.

The validity of a test is all-important. A few independent investigators have found fairly high concurrent validity coefficients between W.I.S.C. scores and achievement tests or other academic criteria of intelligence. As would be expected, the verbal scale tended to correlate higher than the performance scale with such criteria.

Validity is also measured in how far this test assesses the same qualities as represented by other tests of so-called intelligence. The W.I.S.C. and Stanford–Binet I.Q.s have yielded highly correlated results with both pre-school and school-age children ranging in level from mental defective to gifted. As expected, the verbal scale correlated more highly with the Stanford–Binet than did the performance scale. With a test such as the Arthur Performance Scale, on the other hand, the reverse is true, the W.I.S.C. performance I.Q. yielding a higher correlation than the W.I.S.C. verbal I.Q. It is important to note that normal and superior children tend to score higher on Stanford–Binet than on W.I.S.C. and discrepancy in favour of the Binet is greater for brighter and younger subjects. On the other hand, for the mentally retarded the W.I.S.C. yields a significantly higher mean I.Q. than the Binet.

An analysis of occupational differences in verbal, performance and full scale I.Q.s is also of interest in this connexion. When the children in the standardization sample were classified into eight categories in terms of father's occupation, the hierarchy of mean I.Q.s obtained showed a difference of 16 points between the extreme groups in both verbal and full scale I.Q.s, and a difference of 13 points between mean performance I.Q.s. As in all such comparisons, however, the overlapping of distributions for different occupational categories was very large. Individual cases in the lowest category who excel and individual cases in the highest category who fail can easily be found. There was also some evidence that these class differences declined with age, possibly because of exposure to relatively uniform schooling.

The W.I.S.C. as a diagnostic instrument

1. *Classifying intellectual levels* Generally speaking, the W.I.S.C. divisions into seven intellectual groups are recommended for cognitive classification. These can be best illustrated in a table.

W.I.S.C.

Classification	I.Q.	Per cent
Mental defective	69 and below	2·2
Borderline mental defective	70–79	6·7
Dull normal	80–89	16·1
Average normal	90–109	50
Bright normal	110–119	16·1
Superior	120–129	6·7
Very superior	130 and above	2·2

The normal curve range would also include 55 and below, and 145+, each representing approximately 0·14 per cent of the population. Intelligence so measured relates to educational attainment and occupational potential.

2. *Differences between verbal and performance scores* Many W.I.S.C. users attribute meaning to differences between a child's verbal and performance scale scores. Sea-

shore (1951) turned to Wechsler's original standardization data to investigate the meaning of such discrepancies,
while several investigators such as Newman and Loos,
Sloan and Schneider, and Stacey and Levin have published further studies in Littell (1966). In general, it seems
that one should expect mentally retarded children classified as familial or undifferentiated to obtain higher performance than verbal scale scores, whilst those mentally
defective due to brain damage showed significantly *lower*
performance than the undifferentiated groups. On the
other hand, Atchison (1955) found that the eighty feeble-
minded Negro boys and girls he tested tended to score
higher on the verbal scale than on the performance scale,
reversing the differences found above. It would seem safe
to assume that there are important variables involved in
the relationship between verbal and performance scale
scores which were not controlled adequately in the above
studies and much more research is needed before use with
the individual child in the clinic, except with extreme
caution, is recommended.

In a breakdown with reference to occupational categories, verbal/performance (V/P) discrepancies of the
professional and semi-professional classes contain a significantly greater proportion of children with higher verbal
than performance I.Q.s. In this group, 62 per cent had a
positive V/P difference, 35 per cent a negative difference,
and 3 per cent had identical I.Q.s on both scales.

It is now known that differences below 15 points have
little clinical significance in terms of brain damage,
educational retardation and the like, and the younger the
child the more likelihood of a larger discrepancy being
quite normal. Recent normative data supplied by Field
(1960) on V/P discrepancies at different age levels has
been of tremendous value in this area and allows more
precise evaluation. We know what percentage of children
obtain given V/P discrepancies in the normal population
at any given age. For example, at ten-and-a-half years of
age 20 per cent would normally have about a 15 point

difference, and 10 per cent would normally have about a 20 point discrepancy, yet many clinicians use these figures for diagnosing abnormalities such as brain damage. In fact, the statistically 'abnormal' discrepancy at ten years is 23·5 or more.

3. *Patterns of subtest deviations* As one might expect, the almost unlimited possibilities presented by scores on ten subtest areas of intellectual functioning have resulted in numerous hypotheses about how these subscales relate to various aspects of a child's behaviour. The problem of defining a 'significant' deviation between subscales has been widely considered by such people as Alimena and Field from whom tables are now available for assessing significant subtest scatters (Field, 1960; Littell, 1966). In general, any two subjects must differ by at least six points to be clinically and statistically important. Interpreting subtest scores without regard for statistical consideration is a common practice, which should be strongly discouraged, if not banned. Wechsler assumes that specific subtests tap not only general intelligence but specific factors as well. But the exact nature of these factors is far from clear, and no help is given in interpreting the meaning of the subtests of the W.I.S.C., except to state that they seem to measure different factors in children than in adults. There is little recent research to improve the situation.

It would appear that most, if not all, interpretations are based on an intuitive appraisal of the content of the subtest and the informal observations of test adminstrators. While some agreement might be found as to the most likely interpretation of some subtest scores (e.g. digit span), other subtests (e.g. similarities) might produce wide disagreement. Even if one could find agreement as to what a particular item should measure, the question of empirical validation would remain. It should be noted further that most, if not all, of the coefficients of internal consistency would cast much doubt on any individual prediction from individual subtests. In the last analysis it would seem that any prediction made on the basis of an individual subtest score, unless it is statistically based, is little more than a rationalized hunch. A plausible rationale certainly does not make a valid measure.

Organic brain damage

Many clinicians have opinions about, but few well controlled studies have concerned themselves with finding W.I.S.C. subtest patterns characteristic of children with organic brain damage. Beck and Lam in 1955 did investigate the W.I.S.C. records of 104 children referred as possible candidates for a special class for the educable mentally retarded. These children were placed into three groups: (a) organic, diagnosed by neurological examination; (b) suspected organics, inferred by psychological studies; and (c) non-organic, from whom there was no evidence from psychological evaluation or developmental history. From a comparison of the mean verbal, performance and full scale scores and of the inter-subtest scatter, they concluded that (a) organics tend to score lower on the W.I.S.C. full scale than non-organics, (b) organics tend to score lower on the W.I.S.C. performance and full scales than on the verbal scale, (c) the possibility of organic damage increases considerably as the I.Q. drops below the 70–80 range, and (d) *the W.I.S.C. does not show a characteristic pattern of subtest scores for organics as a group*. This typifies the results in this area, though unfortunately clinicians still diagnose 'brain damage' or suspected brain damage all too easily and frequently, and certainly *without* scientific validation.

Reading difficulty

The question of a W.I.S.C. pattern for children with marked reading difficulties has attracted many clinicians. Altus in 1956 reported a distinctive test pattern for children with severe reading disabilities. The records of twenty-five children (twenty-four boys and one girl) who showed a discrepancy of two years or more between their expected and actual reading levels were investigated. Coding and arithmetic subtests were found to be significantly lower than vocabulary, digit span, picture completion, object assembly, and picture arrangement; information was lower than picture completion and digit span. Recent Australian research has confirmed the relationship of coding to reading difficulties. However, with an intelligence test of ten subtests, the chances that at least one subtest would deviate significantly from the mean of *all* of the others is one in ten. This factor takes on particular importance in the above study, for there was no rationale stated prior to the study by which one would expect any particular test to deviate. One cannot, therefore, definitely draw the conclusion that there is a specific W.I.S.C. pattern for poor readers.

Summary

In summary, it should be said the W.I.S.C. has not attained perfection; more study of its validity, the effects of examiner–examinee interaction, repeated administration and the like are vitally needed.

On the other hand, the W.I.S.C. is undoubtedly the best single clinical instrument for measuring intelligence in children and it appears to be a relatively well-standardized test with many virtues. The W.I.S.C. correlates consistently well with other measures of intelligence, appears to be widely accepted and, in general, merits much further research, development and clinical use. Its relatively less frequent use in educational than clinical practice is of particular concern.

W.I.S.C. – short form

Recent developments from the W.I.S.C. have resulted in several extremely useful, accurate short forms of the measure by such workers as Carleton and Strong, and Maxwell. One widely used in Britain is a factorial form produced by A. E. Maxwell (1959) to give verbal, performance and full scale I.Q.s based on four subtests – similarities, vocabulary plus block design and object assembly. This form also provided data on V/P discrepancies scores on the individual child. The Maxwell form is time-saving, efficient and both reliable and valid as a measure of cognitive ability. The child can be classified on a percentile point or in the standard categories of the W.I.S.C. – average (90–109), mental defective (69 and below), superior (120–129) and the like.

Finally, let me stress that despite its limitations the W.I.S.C. full and short forms are the 'best' measures available for assessing intellectual ability in the individual child in the clinic, although in detailed interpretation of the subtest scatters, caution must be exercised. For details of studies mentioned on the W.I.S.C., the reader is referred to Littell (1966).

The Wechsler Pre-school and Primary School Intelligence Scale (Wechsler, 1966)

One cannot close this section without mentioning with delight the most recent appearance of the Wechsler Pre-school and Primary School Intelligence Scale (W.P.P.S.I.). The W.P.P.S.I. test, based on the W.I.S.C., but introducing some new scales such as animal houses, provides for assessing verbal, performance and full scale I.Q., as well as subtest scores for 4- to 6½-year-old children, thus extending the lower age limits to the Wechsler Scales. It is extremely valuable clinically, interesting to young children and should prove a useful tool in future research and practice in intellectual assessment.

Illinois Test of Psycholinguistic Abilities (McCarthy and Kirk, 1961)

Analysis shows that cognitive ability includes factors frequently omitted from intelligence tests. One measure of particular clinical interest in this respect is the Illinois

Test of Psycholinguistic Ability (I.T.P.A.). This measure of linguistic skills is gaining increasing importance and shows much promise. As well as presenting normative data on several aspects of linguistic behaviour, it has the rare advantage of being based on a sound psycholinguistic theory developed by Osgood (1957) and allows proposals for a remedial teaching programme in relation to any assessed deficits. Frostig (1967) uses the I.T.P.A. in conjunction with her own developmental visual perception measures to considerable effect.

The I.T.P.A. has nine subscales. Auditory and visual decoding are measured in tests 1 and 2. Then association between auditory and vocal abilities, and visual and motor relationships are assessed in tests 3 and 4, whilst 5 and 6 measure encoding, the ability to express one's ideas in vocal then motor performance. Test 7 measures auditory-vocal automatic ability; test 8, the assessment of auditory-vocal; and test 9, visual–motor sequencing.

Consequently, a profile of psycholinguistic ability can be obtained which has been found useful in diagnostic problems in children, particularly where speech, educational or organic deficit is suspected. The psycholinguistic profile can be related to intellectual and personality profiles to great advantage in individual cases. One looks forward to more extensive normative, reliability and validity data on this measure. The present norms covering the two-to-nine age range could be most profitably extended. It is, however, notwithstanding its language theory and statistical limitations, a most promising technique for clinical practice and further research.

It must be remembered, finally, that intellectual assessment is almost always complemented by other investigations with the child. Frequently, the important issues revolve round the inter-relations of intellectual ability with other characteristics, rather than the measurement of intellect alone. It must not be forgotten that intelligence tests were devised to measure intellectual abilities and should primarily be used for this purpose. It may be that intellectual functioning abnormalities are related to certain medical diagnostic categories such as brain damage and psychosis, but these cognitive limitations are only part of the picture. It is not surprising then that I.Q. tests are not good at diagnosing accepted medical categories of illnesses. Intelligence is a vital function in itself; abnormality has its own implications for educational progress, job future and the like, and the tests should be used in this way. An I.Q. test may tell you that a child with a particular organic lesion (e.g. a paraplegic spastic) has high or low intellectual ability and one may use this when considering his educational future. It will *not* tell you that he has organic lesions. This is an obvious point, yet many intelligent professional personnel fail to grasp it.

3 Educational Assessment

The assessment of educational attainment in children probably has the longest history in terms of *precursors* of psychometric measurement than any other characteristics to come under the cloak of psychological investigation. However, despite the long experience of educationists in assessing the scholastic levels of children, the problems in this area are in some ways more intense than with the measurement of intellectual level. The contribution of subjectivity in assessment by teachers, the problems of relating attainment in one school to that of attainment in another are extremely difficult issues to unravel. In addition to this, we have the major issue of cultured differences in educational procedures which make the international use of psychometric techniques of educational attainment an even more difficult problem than for the so-called 'cultural free' intelligence tests. Consequently, I will discuss only those educational measures normally used in the United Kingdom in relation to assessment. There are three major sources for the educational attainment and diagnostic measures frequently used by the clinical and educational psychologist, and to a certain extent by educational practitioners. These are the measures standardized and made available by the National Foundation for Educational Research, and the Moray House Tests which are developed by the Scottish Foundation for Educational Research, and privately published work such as the well-known Schonell Educational Attainment and Diagnostic Tests.

As with all measurement, the real problem in educational assessment is that of placing a given person along a single or several dimensions in relation to other people. Commonly, the measurement of number, arithmetic or mathematics, and reading or English levels in children between five and fifteen are the presenting issues for the educational or clinical psychologist. These are the problems to be discussed as they are of major concern to teachers and psychologists in everyday practice. I will outline the main procedures for educational assessment and go on to discuss the inter-relationship between these and tests of intellectual level.

This is an appropriate point at which to do this, for the measurement of educational attainment, though extremely valuable in itself, is even more enlightening when related to the intellectual level and also, eventually, the personality characteristics of a particular child. It may, for example, be found that a child is functioning educationally in the top 25 per cent of the population. One's first assessment from these results may be that this child is an able child who is doing well at school. On the other hand, assessment of intellect may show that the intellectual level of this child is that of the top 3 per cent of the population. Consequently, one may possibly regard this child as underachieving. This is an extremely difficult problem. Underachievement itself may also be related to personality factors, social environment, educational opportunity and many other things. The important thing to remember is that one's concept of educational retardation may not necessarily include only those children functioning at the bottom end of the scale or class. It is tacitly assumed in many circles, and indeed we are officially encouraged to think, that educationally retarded or educationally subnormal children are those with a low I.Q. and comparably low educational attainment. As shown later in this chapter, one can just as easily and meaningfully have a child educationally retarded, even though his level of educational attainment is quite high. In other words, educational retardation is relative to the individual child, related to his or her own intellectual level and educational potential, as well as dependent on a particular level at which he or she is functioning at a given time. Techniques are now becoming available for a more exact assessment of the relationships between educational attainment, intellectual level and personality characteristics relevant to this problem, and will be discussed in a later section.

One important problem in educational assessment is the age at which this can be systematically begun. In our educational system, where children begin school at the approximate age of five years, it often takes some time before one can adequately measure educational attainment. In practice, when the child reaches about the age of seven, the measurement of educational levels, retardation and the like are usually undertaken. The problems of measurement are, in fact, similar to those discussed under the headings of intellect and other aspects of behavioural measurement, so that measures for assessing younger age groups are quite feasible and indeed available.

The National Foundation for Educational Research and other similar bodies have standardized a large number of educational attainment tests for the different age levels, mostly between the ages of seven and sixteen. The statistical properties of the normal curve discussed in relation to intelligence have also been found to be applicable to the assessment of scholastic abilities and the development of standardized educational measures. Scores on these tests are transformed into standard scores so that children from all backgrounds, schools, social conditions and the like may be compared on a fairer and more just basis. In addition, a series of educational measures developed privately by F. S. and Eleanor Schonell (1960) are widely used. First published in 1942, these tests have been revised on a number of occasions and include techniques for the measurement of reading, spelling, English and arithmetic. The importance of these developments are the presentation of normative data for the interpretation of results on an individual basis. In fact, the original normative data of Schonell has been supplemented by a Ministry of Education pamphlet published in 1958, and by standardization in other countries, such as Australia, where Professor Schonell is now Vice-Chancellor of the University of Queensland. I will now present some of the more popular measures in some detail and discuss their uses.

Educational Assessment in Reading and English

Schonell Attainment and Diagnostic Tests of Reading and English (F. S. and Eleanor Schonell, 1960)

Reading attainment tests This is a series of four subtests, the first, Test R_1, is an individual attainment test in word recognition for ages five to fifteen. It is composed of 100 words divided into ten words per year from ages five to thirteen and ten words for the two years fourteen and fifteen. The 100 words were selected from 300 words administered individually to approximately sixty children in each of the ten age groups. They are arranged in continuous order of difficulty, the easiest word being read correctly by 55 per cent of children aged five and the most difficult being read correctly by 45 per cent of children aged fourteen to fifteen. The words have no special connexion with any method of reading teaching. The test appears to be equally useful in schools following the look-and-say, whole sentence, phonic methods, or combined methods. The test has been used repeatedly, even at monthly intervals, to check progress, without any practice effect being detected.

The three tests of reading comprehension (tests R_2, R_3 and R_4) cover successive difficulty levels from age six through to age thirteen. Test R_2 is designed for pupils of reading age six to nine and is scored for speed, accuracy and comprehension. The story to be read is sufficiently interesting to keep average readers of six to nine trying. To its credit, it can also hold the interest of the older backward reader, though the printing and layout are of the type that is usually provided for the younger child. The norms – always weak in reading tests for children near the age at which they begin to read – have been revised by the author to give separate norms, based on a five- to six-year-old's vocabulary, which makes the test more useful.

Tests R_3 and R_4, silent reading tests, consist of a number of paragraphs, each followed by questions, instructions, or multiple choice problems. The questions are very close to those which arise in natural reading situations.

Diagnostic tests. Tests R_5, R_6 and R_7 constitute a set of diagnostic tests aimed at identifying whether or not any or all of a large number of specific difficulties are operative in individual cases. Test R_5 is a diagnostic test of graded words containing most of the common phonic combinations and families. The test consists of two parts. The first sixty words contain combinations of vowels and consonants together with the common vowel digraphs such as ai, ee, and consonantal digraphs like ck, gr, and sh, for example. The last thirty words are polysyllabic and are designed to reveal the testee's ability to read words that require syllabification, such as 'forget' and 'contented'. The test's prime purpose is the diagnosis of weaknesses in the auditory or phonic elements of word recognition.

Test R_6, designed to cover directional attack on words, consists of twelve groups of words. Each group comprises four words which contain the same letters, but in different positions. The test rapidly identifies the pupil who has not stabilized his ability to look at words carefully from left to right and to differentiate among words of similar, but slightly different structure. Test R_7 is directed at weaknesses in the perception of visual patterns of words. Its usefulness is mainly as a supplement to Tests R_1 and R_6.

The diagnostic tests are supported in the Schonell books by brief chapters on the clinical evaluation of the complex factors which may underlie the failures revealed by the tests; these are not, however, all embracing.

As they stand, they provide a convenient and reliable testing kit for the teacher or specialist who is experienced and sensitive. For the learner the tests, particularly the diagnostic tests, require supplementing by more detailed case material.

The Standard Reading Tests (Daniels and Diak, 1960)

The Standard Reading Tests are a very useful series of measures being increasingly used in British circles. The battery consists of twelve tests each with a specific function. A six-monthly assessment of reading on test 1 is recommended (the standard test of reading skill for children with reading ages of five to nine years). If a child's performance on test 1 causes concern, a more detailed diagnosis of the situation can be undertaken by administering tests 2 to 12, which cover abstract figures and sentence copying, and measure perceptual development and hand–eye coordination. A visual discrimination and orientation test, letter recognition, aural discrimination, diagnostic word recognition, oral and picture word recognition, silent prose reading comprehension, graded spelling and a reading experience vocabulary test follow. When more extensive and detailed normative data on each of the tests is available, this series of educational assessment techniques will be of even greater value.

The Watt's Sentence Reading Test 1 (Watts, 1956–60)

The National Foundation for Educational Research for England and Wales, and the Scottish equivalent at Moray House, have standardized numerous reading and English attainment measures which are clinically and educationally valuable. The widely used Watt's Sentence Reading Test 1 will be discussed as an illustration. This test consists of thirty-five unrelated, incomplete sentences for which the subject has to choose the correct word from five alternatives. The items are graded in difficulty and the test is timed over fifteen minutes. The test and its range of difficulty can be illustrated by two examples:

Q 1. Come with me to the shops to buy some (fire, water, stone, sweets, motors).
Q 35. The political dangers of monopoly seem to have been much (exasperated, excised, exaggerated, expropriated, expostulated).

Raw scores 1–35 are converted to standardized scores with a mean 100, S.D. 15, based on a sample of 776 girls and boys aged 7·6 to 11·1 separated in monthly groups. A girl of seven years six months with a score of 20 would have a reading quotient of 115. From this, we know that she is on the 68 percentile point (see page 103) for her age.

The Watt's Sentence Reading Test 1 has a high reliability of between 0·82–0·97 and an interesting system for correcting for chance scores.

This measure is an extremely efficient and sound instrument for group and individual assessment of reading ability, even though it does not cover all aspects.

Schonell Diagnostic English Tests

Finally, Schonell presents Diagnostic English tests covering the areas of English usage, capital letters and punctuation, vocabulary, sentence construction and composition. For all of these tests normative data are now available in terms of the means and S.D.s for each age group between nine and fifteen and for each of the individual measures. This allows a profile of the English attainment of a given child and a diagnostic inventory of educational difficulties in English to be recorded.

Neale Analysis of Reading Ability (Neale, 1966)

Dr Marie D. Neale, formerly of Birmingham University Institute of Education, England, now at Sydney University, Australia, published the *Analysis of Reading Ability* in 1958 and a second edition appeared in 1966. The tests consist of three parallel forms – A, B, C – of graded oral reading passages and three supplementary diagnostic tests. The measures include reading and comprehension as well as diagnostic sound production, auditory discrimination and syllable recognition. The normative data cover the six- to thirteen-year-old age range and qualitative information is recorded on such things as general reading habits and word recognition. The reading material is modern and interesting to children. More use and research publication on its application to clinical problems would be welcome.

Educational Assessment in Mathematics

Schonell Arithmetic Attainment and Diagnostic Tests
(F. S. and Eleanor Schonell, 1960)
The attainment tests are available in mechanical and problem arithmetic for children between seven and fifteen. The diagnostic tests, however, are more commonly used on the child in the clinical situation.

The first four subtests cover 100 basic number combinations in addition, subtraction and multiplication, and ninety combinations in division. In each case the combinations are arranged in approximate order of difficulty. Subtest 5 covers more difficult combinations in the above four processes. These subtests are followed by a series of tests, 6 to 11, in graded addition, subtraction, multiplication and division (three tests in division). The items in subtests 6 to 11 are arranged in very carefully graded steps with four items allotted to each step. For example, in the graded subtraction subtest, the first few items involve subtraction of a single digit number from a two-digit number; in the second four, a two-digit number is subtracted from another two-digit number, and so on. Borrowing is introduced at item 17. Thus, if a sharp increase in the number of errors should take place after item 17, we might with some justification suspect that the child's difficulty was connected in some way with borrowing. The items in the other processes are similarly graded. The last subtest, 12, consists of forty items in mental (or problem) arithmetic, but it is not nearly so useful as the others. It is limited in its use by the fact that it uses the

British system of measurement and that it is rather out-dated. This subtest, however, is not an integral part of the test and in many ways the rest of the test is probably better used without it.

Over all, this Schonell series gives a fairly clear picture of attainment in the various areas of arithmetic and allows weakness to be investigated.

Mechanical Arithmetic Tests (National Foundation for Educational Research, 1949–61)

The National Foundation for Educational Research in England and the Scottish Foundation have published several mathematical attainment tests for both group and individual administration which will be of interest to the reader.

The Mechanical Arithmetic Tests are a most useful series. For example, forms 1A and 1B, parallel tests, were originally devised to match children for scholastic attainment in connexion with research into rewards and punishments. The tests were observed to give a normal distribution at the age range eight-and-a-half to nine-and-a-half years and were standardized on over 5,000 children within that range. They were then published as attainment tests in mechanical arithmetic for ages eight to ten.

These measures (1A and 1B) consist of thirty sums in mechanical (formal) arithmetic and the norms are set out in two useful tables, one giving arithmetic ages and the other standardized scores (mean 100, S.D. 15) for the individual child. The tests have been carefully constructed and adequately standardized on representative samples of English children so that the available norms should be as accurate as is possible with tests of this kind.

The mechanical aspects of arithmetic which are usually covered in British primary schools appear in the tests, but it is particularly important to realize the limitations of this type of test. The test constructors have deliberately re-stricted themselves to sampling only the purely mech-anical elements in arithmetic. Any arithmetical quotient derived from these tests should be used with caution as stress on the mechanical elements in arithmetic teaching varies from district to district. The norms, for example, would not necessarily be applicable to Scotland or in Ireland. Number or arithmetic teaching involves so much more than the mechanical elements stressed here so that if it is desired to measure arithmetic ability in general, they should certainly be supplemented by other less restrictive tests. Even so, the tests give a rough guide to an individual child's ability in arithmetic and are useful in guidance work by psychologists.

Graded Arithmetic–Mathematics Test (Vernon, 1949)

Philip Vernon, Professor of Educational Psychology in the University of London, produced the valuable Graded Arithmetic–Mathematics Test in 1949. It consists of seventy-five questions, the earlier arithmetical, the later including algebra, geometry and trigonometry at levels corresponding to the ages at which these subjects are usually taught in British schools. The item gradient is very steep indeed: the first question requires adding 5 and 3; the last concerns the equations of a parabola. 'Arithmetic–Mathematics ages' are worked out. There are five items for each year of mental age, beginning at 6·0. The A.–M. (Arithmetic–Mathematics) age is therefore six years plus one fifth of a year for each correct response. Time is saved by finding a suitable starting level for each child, and by ending the test as soon as a whole group of five items is failed. The instructions given for this are reasonable and adequate. The reliability (0·88) and the standardization of the test are adequate, though the implication that there is the relationship between A.–M. score and mental or reading age to chronological age is doubtful. In fact, the year of school life a pupil has reached – which is largely a matter of chronological age – must be a considerable factor in determining his score on a test like this.

According to the manual, this test is intended 'primarily

for use in Educational and Child Guidance Clinics, where it is important to know the standing of the child in the main school subjects, as well as his mental age.' The test is well designed for this purpose, enabling the tester to gauge the pupil's level quickly and with the minimum of trouble. The grading it provides is coarse, but it should be adequate for preliminary diagnostic procedures. It should show quickly, for instance, whether a pupil is significantly retarded in arithmetic or mathematics. The test may also be used as a group test for school and class surveys, but not in a competitive situation. Its very wide attainment range also makes it a useful general purpose instrument for survey work, though it will not give fine discrimination at any particular level. It is doubtful, however, if the test can be recommended to class teachers for general use in providing A.–M. ages or quotients which can be entered on cumulative record cards.

One general word of caution is necessary, particularly in number assessment. The rapidly changing approach to teaching mathematics must lead to extra care and investigation by the psychologist before he interprets his results. The test measures must be valid and reliable or new ones developed.

Assessing Educational Retardation

I have outlined some of the methods of assessing educational level – but what of assessing its significance? There are two basic problems here: (i) *when is a given child educationally bright, normal or retarded, say in arithmetic or reading, compared with the normal population?* and (ii) *when is a child significantly bright or retarded educationally in relation to his own intellectual level?*

In practice, a rule of thumb has been used for many years to assess educational retardation. If a child is two or more years behind in reading or arithmetic than his age group (or his own intelligence level where it is known), his situation will probably find the light of day. The mildly retarded child is often less fortunate. Recent research, however, by Fransella and Gerver in the clinic (1965) and Savage and O'Connor (1966) in the schools has improved the situation. It is now possible to screen individuals or groups with certain intelligence and educational measures, and estimate the amount of educational retardation in relation to the intellectual level of an individual child. Fransella provided an equation using the W.I.S.C. and Schonell Reading Measures for predicting the expected reading age of a child of a given intellectual ability. The results of the W.I.S.C. and the Schonell Graded Word Reading Test can be used in the equations below to calculate educational level and retardation, if any.

Multiple Regression Equations (Fransella and Gerver, 1965)

Age	Expected reading age
6 years–9 years	−8·44 + (0·98 chronological age + 0·85 I.Q.)
10 years–12 years	−7·68 + (0·64 chronological age + 0·117 I.Q.)
13 years–15 years	−10·86 + (0·72 chronological age + 0·114 I.Q.)

Savage and his colleagues, as part of a longitudinal study of about 500 Northumberland schoolchildren, have devised a group testing procedure for seven- and eight-year-old children to assess educational retardation in reading and arithmetic. Using the Otis Quick Scoring Mental Ability, the Watt's Sentence Reading and the Schonell Arithmetic Attainment Tests, it is possible to screen large classes at a time and assess the degree of educational retardation in individual cases in arithmetic and reading.

The following regression equations are available (Savage and O'Connor, 1966):

Expected R.Q. (reading quotient) $= 30.84 + 0.653$ I.Q.
Expected A.Q. (arithmetic quotient) $= 49.89 + 0.412$ I.Q.
for age range 6.9 to 7.9 on the above tests.

An example may clarify the position: a seven-year-old boy with an I.Q. on the Otis Mental Ability Test of 110 would be expected to have a R.Q. of:

$$30.84 + (0.653 \times 110) = 102.67$$

on the Watt's Sentence Reading Test. His expected A.Q. using Schonell's tests would be:

$$49.89 + (0.412 \times 110) = 95.21$$

The prediction of abnormality or significant retardation of any obtained R.Q. or A.Q. can be measured as follows:

$$\frac{\text{Obtained R.Q.} - \text{Expected R.Q.}}{\text{S.E. est}}$$

If the same boy obtained a R.Q. of 95:

$$= \frac{95 - 102.67}{19.41}$$

$$= -0.39$$

This does not represent a significant difference between obtained and expected R.Q.s. From this, one might reasonably say that a boy aged seven with an R.Q. of 95 and an I.Q. of 110 is not a significantly retarded reader.

As it is crucial to observe educational retardation as early as possible after a child starts school, the group screening method should be extremely valuable to educational and clinical psychologists. Teachers and doctors could be warned of a child's difficulties early in the day and something done about it in terms of remedial education or other treatment.

4 Personality Measurement

In this chapter I wish to introduce some of the techniques of assessment available outside the normally accepted boundaries of intellectual functioning, specifically those of personality measurement. This is a vital and developing field which is of tremendous importance to our understanding of the individual child as a whole. Furthermore, there have been considerable strides taken in the development of techniques for the measurement of personality characteristics in adults over the past twenty-five years and, in more recent times, the extension of these techniques for use with children has been seen to be most promising. The old adage that it is impossible to measure personality may be said to have reached an advanced stage of disrepute.

For convenience, I will divide the techniques available and in growing use into projective tests and psychometric measures as these two groups of personality assessment techniques have rather different backgrounds and potential.

Projective Techniques

Projective techniques have been developed quite extensively both in the United States and in Great Britain. As you are no doubt aware, they originated from the early work of Herman Rorschach (1921–54), who proposed the Rorschach Projective Test or Psychodiagnostic Plates as a method of diagnosing psychiatric disorders. This test has a literature associated with it probably second to none in psychological personality measurement. Since the early Rorschach days, numerous techniques, all purporting to measure personality characteristics, have been developed using the assumptions of the Rorschach – (1) that it is possible to persuade patients to project their difficulties when presented with ambiguous visual stimuli; (2) that these projections can be meaningfully analysed. Originally, in the Rorschach, ink blots were used but lately more structured situations have been developed. A glance at Buros (1959 and 1965) will show the numerous developments in projective tests, the Blacky Pictures, the Szondi test – to name a few. The Rorschach and the Children's Apperception Test, the two most well known projective measures of personality, are good illustrations of this form of testing.

The Rorschach

The Rorschach has been widely used for children, and workers claim that it is applicable from three years old upwards. There have been some modifications of the original test (Rorschach, 1921) and the scoring techniques applied to this measure are numerous and complicated (Kloper and Kelly, 1942). The Rorschach forum claims it takes three years to train a competent Rorschach analyst.

The Rorschach itself consists of ten symmetrical ink blots. These are presented to the subject individually and scored according to the views of one or other of the Rorschach schools. Broadly speaking, scoring can be divided into three areas: *location*, which is scored W for whole, D for details and S for using the white space around the blots; *determinants*, which are characterized into form (F), colour (C) and shading (K) as well as the combinations of these possibilities; and *content* which includes such things as humans (H), animals (A), objects (O), etc.

This scoring is then interpreted, or should be interpreted, according to Herman Rorschach's original writings, in terms of the *total configuration* and not single responses. It is on the interpretation that one begins to realize the doubtful character of the Rorschach test. Location responses, for example, are claimed by one school to measure I.Q. in terms of the percentage of whole responses (W) and obsessive–compulsive characteristics in terms of detail (D), whilst S, using the white around the picture, shows negativistic attitudes. When one looks at the interpretation of determinants the situation becomes more confusing. Colour responses are supposed to relate to emotionality and impulsiveness, K responses to diffuse anxiety and F responses to intellectual ability or neurotic tendencies depending on one's 'Rorschach school'. Finally, contents are interpreted in such a way that H, human responses, denote anxious, depressed and unintelligent people, symptomatic of psychotic deterioration. Whilst O responses (original, however you may define these) are regarded as related to creativity and intelligence. Poor O responders are said to be schizophrenic or feeble-minded.

The situation can perhaps be summed up by saying that despite several recent faith-shaking reports, the Rorschach remains the most widely used clinical test for the assessment of personality (particularly in America). It is also probably the method on which the opinions of clinicians and psychometricians are most sharply divided. The Rorschach adherents have claimed for it an almost clairvoyant power for revealing structure of motive and emotion, while its more determined critics have regarded it as having little reliability, no validity and worthless as either a clinical or research instrument.

The main problem with all projective tests has not been to get people to project and give information when presented with these stimuli, but to know what to do with the information when you collect it. The most commonly seen notation in relation to projective tests is: *reliability and validity – no data available.* This immediately makes one apprehensive of using projective techniques. One becomes even more concerned when one looks at projective tests that have been subjected to several years of experimental investigation. To quote from two modern reviewers in this area. Professor Eysenck concluded that (1) there was no consistent meaningful theory underlying modern projective devices, and (2) there is no evidence of any relationship between derived projective test scores and outcome of psychotherapy. He advances these conclusions, which are not perhaps different from those obtained by other reviewers such as Cronbach. Lawrence Shaffer, an author quite sympathetic to the Rorschach, has written 'for how many years can a diagnostic method be said to be promising; more than 20 years ago, I concluded one of the earliest descriptions of the Rorschach to appear in America. The Rorschach seemed promising in 1936 ...' but concludes, however, '*it is time psychologists abandoned its beguiling, but dubious orthodoxy and struck out in new directions which will retain some of the demonstrated values, but avoid the numerous pitfalls of unstructured projective techniques*' (Buros, 1959). The present writer cannot recommend the use of this test in clinical practice for measuring children's personality. It may perhaps be used as a method of getting a child to give general information or gain rapport, but the utmost caution should be taken when reading reports based on this test.

Children's Apperception Test (C.A.T.) (L. and Sonya Bellak, 1949–55)

This test, devised by Leopold and Sonya Bellak in 1949 and recently revised, also claims to be useful with children between the ages of three and ten, and is popularly used in child guidance clinics. It is supposed to measure such characteristics as oral conflicts, sibling rivalry and modes of responding to the world. The C.A.T.-S., a supplementary test, measures such things as fears in play, interpersonal problems in classrooms and, believe it or not, fantasies about preganancy in three- to ten-year-olds. In this test the child is given cards with ambiguous pictures. The story responses are recorded and interpreted.

All I wish to say about this test is to quote Dr Kenny

(Buros, 1959), a reviewer and one time sympathetic user of the C.A.T.

In terms of standards applied to measures of intelligence, aptitude and achievement, the C.A.T. and C.A.T.-S. would not be regarded as suitable for operation. Nothing is known about how the story content reflects the deep underlying structure of the child's personality. It is a *clinical, not a psychometric technique*, it gives hunches, no more, no measurement and, needless to say, like most projective tests no data on reliability or validity are available.

The attitude which perhaps exemplifies the present thinking of scientifically oriented psychologists towards the use of projective techniques is that they would not deny that information, sometimes important information, can be derived from a patient using projective techniques. They feel, however, that these techniques must be regarded as being no more than a completely unstructured interview, that attempts to modify these tests along accepted psychometric lines have failed and that their use in clinical practice is rarely, if ever, justified. Although attempts have been made to standardize the stimuli and the scoring procedures, i.e. the pictures or the sentences given to the patient, the interpretive manner in which the results are discussed leaves much to be desired. There may in the past have been some justification for using projective techniques as indeed for many years, particularly with children, no other techniques of measurement of personality were available. This is not the position today and one cannot justify the use of projective tests which are presented without any normative data, without any assessment of their reliability and with no knowledge of their validity in the clinical and educational settings. One must conclude that the information gained through projective tests advances virtually nothing on what can be gained in the normal clinical interview.

Psychometric Techniques

The development of psychometric techniques to measure personality characteristics in children is of very recent origin and stems in the main from the investigations of Professor R. B. Cattell and his colleagues in the Institute of Personality and Ability Testing, Illinois, U.S.A. and Professor H. J. Eysenck's group at the Department of Psychology, Institute of Psychiatry, University of London. Cattell's Children's Personality Questionnaire for ages eight to twelve and High School Personality Questionnaire for ages twelve to sixteen were copyrighted in 1959 and 1962, whilst his Early School Personality Questionnaire for ages six to eight is of even more recent origin (1964). The Junior Eysenck Personality Inventory for seven- to sixteen-year-olds, developed by Sybil and Hans Eysenck, was published only in August 1965. However, as the use of the Cattell and Eysenck tests, particularly in Great Britain, has been rare, and general knowledge of them rather limited, I would like to outline in some detail what these tests can measure and discuss the exciting contribution they may make to the investigation of the individual child.

Junior Eysenck Personality Inventory
(Sybil B. G. Eysenck, 1965)

I will begin with the Junior Eysenck Personality Inventory (J.E.P.I.) as this is a shorter scale measuring only two personality dimensions, extraversion and neuroticism. This scale is a downward extension of the Eysenck Personality Inventory (Eysenck, 1964) and the original Maudsley Personality Inventory (Eysenck, 1959). The test has sixty questions, twenty-four for the scales of extraversion and neuroticism and twelve for the lie scale.

Normative information on extraversion and neuroticism is available for each year group from seven to sixteen and presented for girls and boys separately. Research has shown that the development of these characteristics is different between the sexes over this age range. Generally speaking, the boys are more extraverted than the girls, a finding not unexpected in view of previous adult information. On the other hand, the neuroticism scores for girls increase with age, though no change is seen in boys' scores. A third scale can be derived from this questionnaire. It is intended as a lie scale in order to estimate the reliability–validity of the test. It was found, however, that there is a significant negative relationship between lie scores and age, and some evidence suggests that this score may be related to maturity level in children.

So far, I have described the Junior E.P.I. but made no reference to its background and the reason for its development. This measure has numerous implications for both personality theory and practical policy in education and clinical work with children. In the first place, a number of investigations have shown that there is an important relationship between neuroticism and performance, both in the academic and working situations. To date, the majority of this information is on adults or near adults and was reviewed by Gibbins and Savage (1965). It can be fairly concluded that there is an inverted U-shape relationship between neuroticism and performance and that the optimum level of anxiety for a given task reduces as the complexity level of the task increases. Consequently, it is extremely important in assessing children's attainment and predicting their future in all areas, to be able to measure the degree of neuroticism present at a given time. Similarly, the measurement of extraversion has applied interest. Several studies have now shown that the learning processes in extraverts and introverts differ in certain respects (Eysenck, 1957, 1960). Theoretically, Eysenck (1957) has postulated that extraverts build up inhibition more quickly and dissipate it more slowly than introverts. One of the corollaries of this is that extraverts should be taught in their learning situations to space practice so that inhibition will not build up too quickly and negate performance, whereas introverts are able to work for longer periods without such deleterious effects. This is of interest to workers in the education of normal schoolchildren and in the area of delinquency where learning is an important contributory factor to the development of the individual child.

The reason for this side line on the actual Junior E.P.I. as a personality measure is to illustrate that the measurement of personality characteristics has important repercussions on the 'treatment' or 'handling' of the child in the clinical and educational setting. Finally, as far as the actual test is concerned, I would like to stress the standardization and development procedures – the considerations which allow a test more scientific reliability and validity, which permit the term psychometric measure. Six thousand children covering the age range six to sixteen were investigated before adequate data were available to present this test as a measure of these two personality characteristics. Several years of research were necessary to develop this two-dimensional measure and more work will be needed before it can be considered perfect. It is, however, a distinct improvement on the projective approach to the measurement of personality, in that we now have the reliability, the validity and the normative data available, even though it be on only two characteristics in children, so that we can compare Johnny X on extraversion and neuroticism in the same way, with the comparative precision, as we have been able to do for his intellectual functioning, and we know this assessment of personality may be as intimately related to his future as cognitive or educational appraisal.

Children's Personality Questionnaire (C.P.Q.)

A number of psychometric personality measures have been devised by Raymond Cattell and his colleagues and now measure several characteristics from six years of age to adulthood. I would like to illustrate the Cattell approach to personality description and measurement with reference to the Children's Personality Questionnaire.

The C.P.Q. (Porter and Cattell, 1959) measures a set of fourteen distinct dimensions of personality and, as said earlier, is complementary to the Early School Personality Questionnaire, six to eight (Cattell, 1964) and the High School Personality Questionnaire, twelve to sixteen (Cattell, 1963) as well as the Adult 16 Personality Factor Questionnaire (Cattell, 1962). The dimensions measured are best set out as in Table 1.

Table 1

The Children's Personality Questionnaire –
The fourteen personality dimensions

Trait designation by letter	Technical title * (popular title in parentheses)
A	Schizothymia *versus* cyclothymia (stiff, aloof *versus* warm, sociable)
B	Mental defect *versus* high general intelligence (dull *versus* bright)
C	Dissatisfied, emotional instability *versus* ego strength (emotional, immature, unstable *versus* mature, calm)
D	Phlegmatic temperament *versus* excitability (stodgy *versus* unrestrained)
E	Submissiveness *versus* dominance (mild *versus* aggressive)
F	Desurgency *versus* surgency (sober, serious *versus* enthusiastic, happy-go-lucky)
G	Lack of rigid internal standards *versus* super-ego strength (casual, undependable *versus* conscientious, persistent)
H	Threctia *versus* parmia (shy, sensitive *versus* adventurous, 'thick-skinned')

Trait designation by letter	Technical title* (popular title in parentheses)
I	Haria *versus* premsia (tough, realistic *versus* aesthetically sensitive)
J	Zeppia *versus* coasthenia (liking group action *versus* fastidiously individualistic)
N	Naturalness *versus* shrewdness (simple, awkward *versus* sophisticated, polished)
O	Confident, adequacy *versus* guilt proneness (confident *versus* insecure)
Q_3	Poor self sentiment formation *versus* high strength of self sentiment (uncontrolled, lax *versus* controlled, showing will power)
Q_4	Low ergic tension *versus* high ergic tension (relaxed composure *versus* tense, excitable)

* In both technical and popular titles, the low score pole of the dimension is given to the left, with the high score pole to the right. However, the user should avoid the assumption that a low score is always 'bad' and the high score 'good'. Except for the intelligence dimension (factor B), we almost always find that being at either end of a factor can be good or bad, depending on the criteria against which one is using the factor scores.

This psychometric measure allows the quantitative assessment of the characteristics mentioned in Table 1 and the comparison of an individual child with what is expected of children of his own age group on each of these dimensions. Consequently, the quality (emotional stability, aggressiveness and the like) and degree, amount or percentile point of abnormality or deviation of any characteristic is easily and conveniently seen. An individual child's raw score can be reproduced in terms of a sten score, which is a standard score, or a percentile position. Each factor or personality dimension is represented by six questions and the test is divided into two forms, A and B, with two parts to each. A profile of the child's personality can be drawn and described with accuracy.

The validity and reliability for this test is remarkably high, correlation coefficients being in the region of 0·75 to 0·85. The test is administered individually or can be given in a group. The questions are asked and the subject simply answers appropriately. For example:

When visiting a new building, do you like to have someone show you around ☐ or do you like to find your own way ☐?
Do you have many friends ☐ or just a few good friends ☐?

This test allows a comprehensive personality description in children of a quantitative, highly reliable type with validity in terms of constructs of personality and prediction of outcome of an acceptable level (0.7 to 0.82). It is so devised that standard scores are interpreted in the same way as scores on intelligence tests. Each of the fourteen personality characteristics measured in the test can be interpreted in terms of primary personality traits and have implications for theory of personality as well as for its measurement. It is also interesting to note that Cattell outlines the predictive and diagnostic uses of his test in the school and the clinic. There are numerous regression formulae which allow one to weight each of the characteristics measured and predict success or failure for certain occupations and diagnose accepted clinical abnormalities in personality. Profiles for clinical groups such as neurotics, psychopaths, psychosomatic disorders and so on are given, as well as information about personality and success in athletics, academic performance and various job situations, etc.

There would seem to me to be no doubt that the C.P.Q. is the most comprehensive, reliable, valid, well-standardized children's personality test available. It has the added advantage of measuring a wide range of personality characteristics and of being related to a sound theoretical and empirical basis (Cattell, 1965). In conjunction with his tests for older and younger age groups, it allows developmental studies as well as individual studies at a given time, and I feel it is, and will be, of immense value. I might add that a form for the measurement of personality in two- to six-year-olds is in the advanced state of research development.

Social Development

Before concluding this chapter on personality, I would like to introduce briefly the measurement techniques related to the widely used concept of social maturity. There are several psychometric measures in this area: I will mention two of them, the Vineland Social Maturity Scale (Doll, 1947) and the Bristol Social Adjustment Guides (Stott, 1963).

In 1947, Dr Doll and his colleagues at the Vineland Institute, U.S.A., developed the Vineland Social Maturity Scale which assesses various aspects of social development. The scale allows us to assess the individual child in relation to other children (and adults) in terms of a social maturity quotient, as well as giving subgroups' scores on self-help generally, self-help eating, self-help dressing, self-direction, occupation, communication, locomotion and socialization. The test was originally standardized on 620 subjects virtually from birth to adulthood and some recent work by Dr L. W. Kellmer-Pringle (1966) has done much to improve the normative data and interpretative material for British groups. Normative data on the subclasses is still not available, so a social maturity quotient comparable with a Binet I.Q. is the only reliable score obtained from the measure. It is, however, an extremely useful technique for it can be answered by a parent, close relative, or nurse on the child's behalf when the child itself is unable or unwilling to co-operate. The technique has two major uses, firstly as a measure of intelligence with very young children and secondly, when social maturity and intelligence levels can be compared. High grade mental defectives and E.S.N. children may show considerably higher social maturity than intellectual level. I recommend Kellmer-Pringle's short paperback *Social Learning and Its Measurement* to any interested in this area.

A rather different test of social development – the Bristol Social Adjustment Guides – was published by Stott and his colleagues in 1963. These scales are of two major types, those referring to the child in the school and in residential care (boy and girl versions) and those referring to the child in the family. The scales have been widely used in relation to delinquency, school and home problems with children.

Both the Vineland Social Maturity Scale and the Bristol Social Adjustment Guides may be filled in by parents or persons familiar with the child – a distinct advantage with handicapped or difficult children.

I hope that this brief introduction to personality assessment will be of value and encourage a more scientific approach to this problem by psychologists, educational and medical practitioners, as well as the lay public.

5 Motor and Perceptual Development

The area of motor development is one of the most under-privileged in psychological literature (Savage, 1965). On the other hand, in the clinical and educational fields the problem of assessing motor development is a persistent and difficult one – for example, with spastic children, both for their educational and occupational future. The major difficulty in assessing motor behaviour is the paucity of normative data in this area, particularly in relation to more refined motor abilities. One must acknowledge the great debt to Gesell and Ilg, Griffiths and Illingworth in standardizing the development milestones in motor as well as other capacities. In addition, most of the psychometric techniques such as Griffiths' Scale, the Merrill-Palmer, the Minnesota Pre-school Scales, the Vineland Social Maturity Scale, the Binet and the W.I.S.C. include aspects of motor development, but are basically measures of more general intellectual capacities in children. However, the measurement of motor ability and of motor learning, as distinct from intellectual and other characteristics, has been greatly neglected. There are few standardized motor tests available yet a great deal of information on motor skills and motor learning from experimental psychology which has a promising future in its application to the clinical assessment of motor deficiencies in children. In this chapter, I wish to present some information on standardized tests of motor and perceptual development which may be of interest to people working in clinical and research fields.

General Motor Measures

Scanning the main sources of psychological test information edited by Buros (1959, 1965 and 1961), one will find only two over-all tests of motor development: the Lincoln–Oseretsky Motor Development Scale, the latest version of which has been standardized by Sloan (1955) in America, and the Brace Scale of Motor Ability (Brace, 1927). In addition, there are a number of more limited motor tests covering coordination, steadiness, laterality, tapping, and several manual dexterity measures.

The Brace Scale of Motor Ability (D. K. Brace, 1927)

The Brace Scale of Motor Ability is an interesting one used mainly in relation to normal children and physical educational programmes, rarely, in the clinical situation. This scale, first published in 1927, was designed to measure that ability which is 'more or less general ... more or less inherent, and which permits an individual to learn motor skills easily.' It has been extensively used in physical education programmes to classify students into homogeneous groupings for activity. Because it was designed to measure such aspects of motor ability as agility, balance, control and flexibility and to minimize the importance of size and strength, it is more valuable in classifying students for individual activities than for team sports. It is especially applicable to programmes emphasizing gymnastics, tumbling, dancing (modern and folk), diving and games needing little organization. This test, its derivatives and extensions, are probably the best screening devices available in physical education for the identification of difficulties in gross motor coordination.

The original scale consists of thirty-nine tasks, all of which involve active manipulation of the entire body. Each requirement is clearly described by the instructions to the subject. No equipment and very little space is required. Scoring is in terms of success or failure. Specific statements of what constitutes failure are given. For example:

Test 1

> Walk in a straight line, placing the heel of one foot in front of and against the toe of the other foot. Start with the left foot. Take ten steps in all, five with each foot. *Eyes open.*

Failure: (a) Losing the balance and stepping out of line, (b) not walking in a straight line, (c) not placing heel to toe.

This measure is appropriate for both sexes throughout the school system (five to eighteen years) and older children may score each other in a group testing situation, so that a class of forty can complete the test in about forty-five minutes.

The Iowa–Brace Scale

Revisions of the Brace Scale, called the Iowa–Brace, by McCloy and Young (1954) and Vickers, Payutz and Baum (1942) were designed to minimize still further the importance of strength, power, maturity and size, but at the same time to show improvement with age. Separate batteries of ten tests each are presented for elementary school boys and girls, junior high school boys and girls, and senior high school boys and girls.

The Brace and Iowa–Brace correlate approximately 0·75. The latter is only half of the former and, as might be expected, is somewhat less reliable. The two tests are obviously similar, however, and if a quick rough measure in a practical situation is desired, the shorter Iowa–Brace will be appropriate. Norms are available for each age year.

These scales administered individually or to small groups are valuable practical and research tools for the study of gross motor ability. Reliabilities are very high and test correlations at intervals of six months were found to be between 0·9 and 0·87 for children five to nine years of age, and 0·77 to 0·88 and 0·53 to 0·72 for secondary school girls and boys respectively.

The scale was validated originally against judgement

ratings of physical education teachers and a battery of athletic events. The Brace and its derivatives are primarily for use in the normal school. A report on their use on British schoolchildren was published by Bill (1958).

The Lincoln–Oseretsky Motor Development Scale (Sloan, 1955)

It would seem that the Lincoln–Oseretsky scale is the only standardized motor proficiency scale at present used in the clinical situation to any great extent. Even so, its use in Great Britain is limited (at least if one takes the number of clinical or research reports on the topic into consideration). I would recommend the use of this scale in any programme designed to assess the child with suspected motor deficiencies, whether these are inherited, the result of neurological damage or whose aetiology is unknown.

The scale was originally developed in Russia and first used in Western Europe in the form of a Portuguese translation which was later available in English. The original scale was set out very much like the Binet Intelligence Scale in that a certain number of items per age group were given and a motor development quotient calculated in relation to motor age and chronological age. In 1955, William Sloan modified and standardized the Lincoln–Oseretsky scale on an American population. It now consists of thirty-six items arranged in order of difficulty. It is an extremely efficient measure which allows the assessment of the individual child and permits a precise statement of his or her motor development as compared with other children. The manual describes a complete analysis of results obtained on 380 boys and 369 girls, six to fourteen years of age, on each item retained in the Sloan scale. Percentages passing each item at each level, validity, reliability and tentative percentile norms for the sexes, separately and combined, are given.

About two thirds of the items consist of hand and arm movements measuring speed, dexterity, coordination and rhythm. The remainder are gross motor items – seven of these involve balance and four jumping.

What does this motor test measure? Oseretsky claimed that his scale measures static coordination, dynamic coordination and, in general, speed of movement and asynkinesia, but no statistical support of this analysis was ever published. However, later factor analyses of Lincoln–Oseretsky scores on 211 boys, seven-and-a-half to eleven-and-a-half years of age, found only one common factor accounting for about 20 per cent of the variance of the measure. It was thought to be one of motor development as it also correlated 0·70 with age. Sloan (1955) reported low correlation of scores on this test with gross motor tests, indicating that the Lincoln–Oseretsky does not measure strength or power. It can quite properly be called a scale of motor development, since the items sample a variety of motor performance and the scores improve with age. From this test a motor score and a motor development quotient can be calculated.

The Sloan Lincoln–Oseretsky is particularly useful as a base line for the investigation of motor difficulties. One has a motor development quotient which may be compared with intellectual level and so on to assess not only the child's position relative to other children in relation to motor development, but also to assess his motor development in relation to his intellectual and scholastic attainment, and finally in relation to his social–occupational success and/or potential.

The limitations of the Oseretsky scale relate to its generalized nature. In many ways, it is like comparing the Binet and Wechsler Intelligence Scales: in the former, one has an overall measurement of intellectual ability, in the latter, a more precise analysis of this cognitive ability into subareas. The Oseretsky is the Binet of motor development. What we now need is its W.I.S.C. equivalent. We need, in fact, subscores on the factors which go to make up general motor development, manual dexterity, left arm, right arm, both, use of the legs separately and in coordination, general posture, perceptual motor co-ordination and so on. However, one should not under-estimate the importance of the Oseretsky scale and future development of it could no doubt remedy many of its deficiencies. From the clinical point of view, it is an easily administered scale (provided the psychologist has a rea-sonable motor ability) and one enjoyed very much by children. It is particularly useful, I think, in relation to the assessment of that group of children classified some-times as 'clumsy children' who present a limited motor disfunction which may have an important bearing on their education and occupational future.

Specific Motor Measures

Several techniques which may be termed psychometric, though not yet perhaps thoroughly standardized, are also of interest in this area of motor functioning. I would like to discuss the Purdue Pegboard (Tiffin, 1941–48), the original purpose of which was to aid in selecting em-ployees for industrial jobs requiring manipulative dex-terity and intended to measure both gross movements of arms, hands and fingers, and 'tip of the finger' dexterity, and the Heath Rail Walking Test (Heath, 1942, 1949) as examples of those more limited or more specific tests of motor ability.

The Purdue Pegboard (Tiffin, 1941–48)

This manual dexterity test is made of wood and contains two rows of twenty-five holes into which pins can be inserted. At the top of the board are four cups containing pins, washers and collars to be assembled. No tools are employed.

The test involves two types of operations. One requires rapid placing of pins in the holes and it is scored for each hand separately, for the sum of right and left hand scores, and for alternating right and left hand movements. There is a time limit of thirty seconds for each trial. The other operation requires the assembly of pins, washers and collars using both hands. The score is the number of components assembled in each one-minute trial.

A profile sheet provides spaces for recording scores and norms for converting scores to percentiles. Male and female norms are available for one-trial and for three-trial totals, computed to take into account the improvement resulting from practice. The reliability data reported in the manual indicate that test–retest correlations for the one-trial administration range from 0·60 to 0·76 with a median of 0·68.

Recently this test has been used in relation to brain-damaged children by Rapin and his colleagues and an attempt made to collect normative data on children with regard to this measure of manual dexterity. I prefer this test to be used as a measure of manual dexterity rather than a potential brain-damage diagnostic test. Nevertheless, more normative data and information on its reliability and validity in relation to occupational success, for example, by spastic and normal children would be invaluable.

Rail Walking Test (Heath 1942, 1949)

In order to show that there are also possibilities in relation to the assessment of non-manual motor ability, I would like to mention Heath's Rail Walking Test which has been available since 1942. This test usually employs two 9 foot long rails, 14 and 12 inches wide and a 16 foot long rail, 1 inch wide. It is given in an untimed form, the subject being required to walk along it in his stockinged feet. The Rail Walking Test has been extensively standardized by Heath and has a high reliability. It can therefore be used in assessing the individual child in relation to balance, etc.

Heath discovered an adjustment syndrome, characterized by poor motor coordination among other things, was an important contributor to scores on this test, and the possible relationship of this lack of motor coordination to neuroticism was confirmed later by the work of Tizard,

O'Connor and Crawford (1950). Using it along wıtn a number of other tests, they found that it had a significant loading on the neuroticism factor which resulted from their factorial analysis. Unfortunately too little work has since been carried out with specific motor tests on normal, psychiatric or spastic groups of children. I would like to see more systematic use of them in the assessment of a child's motor ability. Furthermore, though applied psychology has been particularly tardy in its development of motor tests, an interest in motor skills and motor learning has been with us for some years in relation to both experimental psychology and what may broadly be called industrial psychology. A great deal of work has been done to develop apparatus and methods of measuring particular aspects of motor skills, motor learning and so on, but too little has been applied and many problems still remain unanswered.

One of the puzzling issues in this field has been the question of the specificity or generality of motor ability. Early work in the field suggested that the ability to do one type of motor task was relatively independent of the ability to do any other, and this may well have held up research and application in this area. Recent work reviewed by Yates (1960) and other writers suggests that a general factor of psychomotor ability cannot be doubted, but that groups of motor abilities also exist. For example, Fleishman (1954) has analysed ten independent group motor factors. They include: (i) wrist–finger speed, (ii) finger dexterity, (iii) wrist to arm movement, (iv) aiming, (v) aim under steadiness, (vi) reactive time, (vii) manual dexterity, (viii) psychomotor speed, (ix) psychomotor coordination, and (x) spatial relations. Though these factors may not be regarded as the exclusive ones, they are obviously of vital importance and should lead to the development of more precise factorially based measures of motor ability, perhaps a motor equivalent of the W.I.S.C.

In the experimental investigations of motor development, a number of interesting techniques have been developed. The tracking apparatus, I think, is worth particular mention as it has wide use. It has been said that the tracking apparatus is to the measurement of human motor abilities as the Skinner box is to the animal laboratory. You can study anything with it, for it can range from a simple paper and pencil maze to an electronically operated driving or flying simulator, yet it is virtually unknown in the clinic. Consider some of the possibilities: psychometrically, it could be used as a measure of motor coordination, to measure motor learning and fatigue, to assess motor transfer ability and the like. Furthermore, children normally find motor learning tasks interesting and challenging. Much more work is needed in this area.

Finally, in Newcastle upon Tyne we are in the early stages of developing a Motor Learning Test for diagnosing learning difficulties associated with brain damage, which has important implications for assessment. Alas, lack of funds limits the speed of development of a W.I.S.C. type of factorially based motor scale (Savage, 1965).

The Bender Gestalt Visual Motor Measures (Bender, 1938)

The original Bender Gestalt, called the Visual Motor Gestalt Test, was published in 1938 and is available for use with patients from over four years of age to adulthood. It was republished in 1951 (Pascal and Suttell, 1951) and revised for those over seven years of age (Hutt and Briskin, 1960). A Bender Visual Motor Gestalt Test specifically for children aged seven to eleven was published by Aileen Clawson in 1962 and the most recent Bender Gestalt Test development for young children five to ten was made available by the work of Elizabeth M. Koppitz in 1964. It consists of eight designs which are copied by the child under standard conditions and scored in as specific a way as possible for errors in reproduction. This test has had wide clinical use, particularly in the U.S.A., but also in Britain. It is popular for its simplicity and speed of administration, the claims for its diagnostic usefulness with emotional and brain-damaged children and its possibilities in relation to I.Q.

The claims for the Bender Gestalt, however, are more impressive than the results. It has undoubted potential, if not merit, as a test of certain aspects of visuo-motor performance, but its success as a clinical diagnostic instrument for emotional and brain-damaged children is very meagre. It is based on clinical intuition rather than scientific fact. It may be used clinically for hunches, but has far from accepted reliability or validity. Much more research is needed before the results of this test can be accepted for individual children; particularly in relation to suspected emotional and brain-damage problems. On the other hand, it can be accepted as a useful clinical tool in relation to intellectual assessment for children four to twelve and an interesting, reliable, scorable test to measure visuo-motor normality and abnormality, provided more normative data are forthcoming.

The Minnesota Percepto-Diagnostic Test
(Fuller and Laird, 1963)

A recent addition to this area, the Minnesota Percepto-Diagnostic Test by Fuller and Laird is of some interest. The M.P.D.T. is standardized on 500 children and 750 adults. It consists of six Gestalt designs which the subject copies; it scores the degree of rotation of design which is then related to schizophrenic, emotional and organic disabilities in children. The problems of this area, however, are far from resolved and uses of this and similar tests must be extremely guarded. At present it may be regarded as an interesting motor–perceptual measure of rotation of designs which may well be related to educational learning difficulties, especially reading and possibly emotional and organic impairment in the child. More research is needed on these perceptual–motor tasks. A very recent revised edition by Fuller (1967) is most welcome.

The Benton Visual Retention Test

This is an individual test devised according to the manual of the revised Visual Retention Test by A. L. Benton (1963) as a 'clinical and research instrument to assess memory, perception and visuo-motor functions'. In fact, it measures memory for designs rather than general memory. The test consists of three drawing forms, each of ten designs. Norms are presented for each form of administration for patients from eight years to old age, and follow a rise to a plateau at fourteen to thirty then a descent. Children's norms for each age year between eight to fourteen, taking into account I.Q. level, are presented. The interpretation of quantitative data such as omissions, rotations and size distortions is discussed. The test is claimed to be particularly useful with children suspected of having cerebral damage who show more defective performance. Emotionally disturbed children, as with the Bender Gestalt, show impaired performance on this test, but cannot as a group or individually be distinguished from normal children. Performance is significantly related to I.Q. which along with other considerations leads one to believe the test would be better used as a memory-for-designs measure than a diagnostic categorizer. In the former capacity, it is of great interest, for this facility is potentially vital to many forms of behaviour and adjustment. Much more research is needed to untangle all the possibilities. It must still be regarded as an experimental test and caution pervade its use in the clinic.

In general, the visuo-motor performance and memory tests are of great interest. However, their reliability and validity, particularly the latter, must be seriously questioned. Used as measures of certain behaviour factors, i.e. visual perception, visual design, memory, etc. they have potential; used as diagnostic indices of emotional or brain-damaged conditions, they have not proved themselves.

The recent increasing use in this area of the Marianne

Frostig Development Test of Visual Perception (1961–64) for pre-school and clinical assessment in school children has promising possibilities. It is reasonably standardized and useful in screening those children who may need special perceptual training in five important areas of visual perception which may well be related to educational difficulties and brain damage.

6 Individual Psychometric Investigations

In the previous chapters, a number of psychometric techniques have been introduced to the reader. This final section is devoted to illustrating the use of these measures with the individual child. As will be realized by now, psychometric assessment is a long, but thorough business, to be practised only by experienced and well-trained applied psychologists. It takes about six years from entrance to university before full professional recognition is possible. This book will not qualify you in the psychometric assessment of children, but it should make the use of these techniques and results from them more meaningful.

There follow some of the problems encountered and investigations performed by the applied psychologist in his everyday work.

The Mental Defective Child

To the modern applied psychologist one of the least technically difficult, but more tragic diagnostic problems, is the investigation of mental deficiency. In any particular case, a suitable intelligence test is used, indeed more than one assessment is often undertaken. Cognitive or intellectual mental deficiency has many causes – genetic or inherited, birth injury, accident and the like – but may be defined in a child whose intellectual quotient is below 70. There are various grades or classifications of mental deficiency with I.Q.s between 69 and levels too low to be measured.

Case 1: slow development

Referral This boy aged four years and eight months was referred to the applied psychological clinic by a consultant paediatrician. His developmental milestones, such as crawling, walking, talking, were not noticeably different from those of the normal child. It was thought that he might have been partially deaf, but audiometric investigation showed this not to be. On the other hand, the child's general behaviour on the ward suggested possible mental retardation.

Psychometric investigation The Stanford–Binet Intelligence Scale was administered to this child, as this measure allows more precise investigation of the lower limits of intelligence with children below school age than, for example, the W.I.S.C.

This particular patient was extremely cooperative during the session. He obtained an I.Q. of 52 which places him well within the mentally defective range. Since intellectual assessment in young children is difficult, a second investigation in about twelve months was recommended, even though in this particular case the low level of intelligence leaves little doubt as to the reliability of the finding. The need for special training-school education for this child was recommended.

Case 2: poor school record

Referral This was a child ten years and six months old. She was referred via her general medical practitioner and paediatrician because of doing rather badly at school and being very babyish in her behaviour.

Psychometric investigation In this case the W.I.S.C., which allows a thorough assessment for a child of this age, was used:

Full scale I.Q. 59
Verbal I.Q. 63   *Performance I.Q. 61*

Verbal scales   *Performance scales*

Information	5	Picture completion	6
Comprehension	3	Picture arrangement	5
Similarities	4	Block design	5
Arithmetic	4	Object assembly	2
Vocabulary	5	Coding	4

Behaviour This young girl was quite cooperative during the testing, which she seemed to enjoy. She was pleasant and chatty, frequently interrupting the proceedings to tell stories about her family and activities at home.

Assessment The full scale I.Q. of 59 falls within the mentally defective range. There was no significant discrepancy between the verbal (63) and performance (61) I.Q. levels, both of which show mental deficiency, nor was the subtest scatter abnormal.

Recommendations The child may be regarded as a high grade mental defective. She would undoubtedly benefit from special training and eventually may be able to live a useful community life within the limits of her intellectual potential.

Continuous investigation, at least at yearly intervals, should be made to check her progress and eventually advise on vocational possibilities. Further intellectual and non-intellectual investigations of her cognitive characteristics and potential are also advised.

It may surprise many that a case of this kind did not come to our attention much earlier in her development. It is most unfortunate but not unusual for children to obtain their first thorough psychometric assessment much too late in their lives for optimal remedial treatment, even though the position is improving in most areas.

The Child with Suspected or Actual Brain Damage

This type of problem child is a recurring one for the applied psychologist. Cognitive and personality difficulties may be present in the patient. These patients are frequently our most difficult for too often the referring consultant wants us to diagnose brain damage but psychometric techniques cannot always, *if ever*, do this, as I have tried to point out. They can, however, make the valuable contribution of assessing the abilities and characteristics of the individual child, brain-damaged or not, and making appropriate recommendations.

Case 3: accident

Referral A six-year-old boy was admitted to the hospital after receiving a blow on the head when falling from a swing. He had on this occasion become unconscious; unconsciousness had also occurred previously after even minor bumps on the head. The child appeared to the hospital staff to be extremely shy and mentally retarded, even though there was no sign of medical physical illness.

Psychometric investigation It was decided in the first place to assess cognitive level and educational attainment in this child. The W.I.S.C. and some of the Schonell Diagnostic Tests were administered.

Full scale I.Q. 94
Verbal I.Q. 89   *Performance I.Q. 101*

Verbal scales		*Performance scales*	
Information	6	Picture completion	6
Comprehension	7	Picture arrangement	10
Arithmetic	10	Block design	9
Similarities	7	Object assembly	12
Vocabulary	11	Coding	14

Schonell Word Reading Test: R.Q. 83.
Schonell Spelling Test (Form A): S.Q. (Spelling Quotient) 97.

Arithmetic (Assessment from W.I.S.C. subscale): A.Q. 100.

Behaviour During the examination the child was attentive and very cooperative.

Assessment The boy's overall cognitive ability (I.Q. 94) is within the normal range (90–109) and there is no significant difference between his verbal and performance I.Q.s which might have resulted had brain injury followed his falls. His scholastic attainments in reading, spelling and arithmetic are consistent with his intellectual ability. The patient's performance on these measures do not indicate any serious repercussions from his accidents. A further appointment should be given to re-investigate the child in about twelve months to check his progress.

Case 4: behaviour problems

Referral This child was referred as suspected of brain damage because of severe behaviour problems and a birth history and development not inconsistent with damage to the cerebral cortex.

Psychometric invesigation 1 Initially the W.I.S.C., the Bender Visual Motor Gestalt Koppitz version and the Minnesota Percepto-Diagnostic Tests were given to assess cognitive functioning with possible organic involvement.

W.I.S.C.
Full scale I.Q. 96

Verbal scales I.Q. 96		*Performance scales I.Q. 97*	
Information	11	Picture completion	10
Comprehension	6	Picture arrangement	7
Arithmetic	9	Block design	13
Similarities	9	Object assembly	10
Vocabulary	12	Coding	8
Digit span	9		

Bender Visual Motor Gestalt (Koppitz): Score 0 (within normal range).
Minnesota Percepto–Diagnostic Test: Score 49 (within normal range).

Behaviour 1 The patient was cooperative during testing and there were no indications of abnormal distractability of attention span.

Assessment 1 His over-all intelligence was within the average range. There was no W.I.S.C. verbal–performance discrepancy, nor any unusual subscale scatter indicative of abnormal organic involvement or basis for his cognitive functioning. The Bender Gestalt and Minnesota Tests' scores measuring motor–perceptual performance in reproducing designs were normal and did not indicate that organic damage may have affected these functions.

Recommendations 1 Further psychometric investigation of educational attainments and personality characteristics may shed some light on the behaviour problems of this child which may or may not be organically based. His cognitive functioning appears normal, however, as there is no evidence of the cognitive functioning abnormalities associated with brain damage.

Psychometric investigation 2 Some of the Schonell Scholastic Diagnostic Measures and the Cattell Children's Personality Questionnaire were administered.
Schonell Graded Word Reading Test: R.Q. 118.
Schonell Diagnostic English Tests: English Usage Quotient 117, Punctuation Quotient 90.
Schonell Mechanical Arithmetic Test: A.Q. 79.

Cattell Children's Personality Questionnaire

Factor		Sten score
A	Outgoing, warmhearted	3
B	Intelligence	7
C	Emotional stability	4
D	Excitability, overactive	9
E	Dominance	6
F	Happy-go-lucky	2
G	Super-ego strength	2
H	Socially bold	3
I	Sensitivity	6
J	Doubting, individualistic	7
N	Shrewdness	9
O	Guilt-proneness	10
Q_3	Self-disciplined	4
Q_4	Tenseness	6

Behaviour 2 Once again, this child was quite cooperative during the assessment sessions.

Assessment 2: scholastic attainment This child's reading ability and grammatical English usage are generally in line with his intellectual level and if anything are slightly better than expected. On mechanical punctuation and capitals his performance is poor, but not seriously so. It could be improved. His A.Q. 79 does, however, fall below the expected level and shows underachievement for this child.

Assessment 2: personality measurement This patient has a fairly high level of general anxiety on the second order factor (on the 75 percentile point), but he was not particularly extraverted. The results on the specific factors A to Q_4 are consistent with his history, particularly his abnormal behaviour. On super-ego strength his score is in the bottom 6 per cent of the population and he is shown to be extremely guilt-prone (97 percentile) suggesting that his anti-social impulses are followed by guilt and depressive reactions. The quality of his behaviour is also indicated by his high excitability and shrewdness, made up of calculating, penetratingly wordly traits. He is shown to have a low esteem for others (factors A and H) and a basically unstable and difficult personality.

Recommendations 2: His personality difficulties appear important as no cognitive abnormalities were evident. Sustained psychiatric and psychological help is required for this child in view of his personality characteristics and some educational assistance, especially in arithmetic, recommended.

Case 5: actual brain damage

Referral This child was referred from a neurosurgical department after treatment for severe head injuries following a motor car accident at the age of twelve years. He was being difficult to handle at home, aggressive and doing badly at school. Prior to the accident, he had been an average child at home and school and had given no trouble.

Psychometric investigation In this case, several sessions were necessary to examine the many characteristics of the child and to look for possible evidence of the effects of organic damage received in the accident.

W.I.S.C.
Full scale I.Q. 75

Verbal I.Q. 100		*Performance I.Q. 53*	
Verbal scales		*Performance scales*	
Information	10	Picture completion	4
Comprehension	7	Picture arrangement	5
Similarities	11	Block design	3
Arithmetic	10	Object assembly	2
Vocabulary	11	Coding	2
Digit span	12		

Verbal/performance (V/P) discrepancy 47.

The Bender Visual Motor Gestalt Test (Koppitz): unscorable.
The Minnesota Percepto-Diagnostic Test: unscorable.

Cognitive assessment The overall cognitive level (I.Q. 75) of this boy is in the borderline mental defective range (70–79). His level of achievement must therefore be limited by this, despite his average verbal I.Q. The situation is aggravated by the significant V/P discrepancy of 47 points which is indicative of cognitive loss resulting from the accident. The indication of significant organic damage effect on cognitive functioning is further supported by the abnormal (organic) scores on the two motor–perceptual tests, the Bender Gestalt and Minnesota Measures which were so poor as to be unscorable.

Recommendations There would seem no doubt that the head injuries from the accident have had a significant effect on this child and his future attainment. He cannot be expected to function above the borderline mental defective or educationally subnormal level and will need special education.

Further psychometric investigation is recommended to measure his present educational levels, personality characteristics and detailed 'memory' assessment so that his progress may be charted at intervals to allow appropriate action.

The Educationally Retarded Child

The problem of educational development of the child and its assessment is a perennial one for the applied psychologist. The number of children, especially between ten and thirteen, referred as school problems by paediatricians and school doctors is quite high. Investigation of these children should take place much earlier in their educational career. Two referrals, however, will illustrate the major types of educationally retarded cases.

Case 6: educational and intellectual retardation

Referral This young girl of seven years was referred for assessment due to backwardness at school noticed originally by the teacher and parents.

Psychometric investigation The Stanford–Binet Intelligence Scale was administered and the Schonell Graded Word Reading and Mechanical Arithmetic tests given:
Stanford–Binet: I.Q. 84.
Schonell Graded Word Reading Test: R.Q. 85.
Mechanical Arithmetic Test: A.Q. 85.

Assessment This child's cognitive ability is within the dull-normal range (80–89) and her R.Q. and A.Q. each of 85 are consistent with her intellectual level. Though they may be slightly below average for her age group, she is not significantly retarded, nor is she functioning below her own expected level. She should cope in a normal school, though in the lowest levels of ability.

Case 7: educational underachievement

Referral The following child was referred because of concern about her scholastic attainment. She had lost some, but not a great deal of schooling because of asthmatic illness, and had been educated in a small country school.

Psychometric investigation 1 The short form of the W.I.S.C. was first given to find her base line intellectual level followed by personality and educational assessment. W.I.S.C. (Maxwell Short Form).

Full scale I.Q. 118

Verbal I.Q. 111		*Performance I.Q. 134*	
Verbal scales		*Performance scales*	
Similarities	11	Block design	15
Vocabulary	13	Object assembly	17
V/P discrepancy	23		

Cattell Children's Personality Questionnaire

Factor		Sten score
A	Outgoing, warmhearted	5
B	Intelligence	8
C	Emotional stability	7
D	Excitability, overactive	4
E	Dominance	4
F	Happy-go-lucky	3
G	Super-ego strength	7
H	Socially bold	7
I	Sensitivity	5
J	Doubting, individualistic	3
N	Shrewdness	1
O	Guilt-proneness	4
Q_3	Self-disciplined	7
Q_4	Tenseness	8

Psychometric investigation 2 Schonell Diagnostic Tests
Arithmetic: addition quotient 110, subtraction quotient
102, multiplication quotient 92, division quotient 95.
English: English usage 108, capitals and punctuation 100.

Behaviour Throughout both sessions she was extremely
cooperative, exhibiting a shy but mature approach to the
situation. In the first session there was a certain amount of
asthmatic difficulty in terms of wheezing and heavy breath-
ing. In the second session she was perfectly normal.

Assessment: intellectual and scholastic attainment Intellectually, this child is over all at the top end of the bright–
normal range (110–119). There is, however, a significant
discrepancy (23 points) between her verbal I.Q. (111) and
performance I.Q. (134) which would suggest that she may
be underfunctioning in an educational setting. Subsequent
assessment of educational level with the Schonell Diagnostic English and Arithmetic Tests supported this
assumption of educational underachievement. Educationally she is functioning only within the average range, both

in English and arithmetic. One would expect a child of her overall intellectual level, and particularly in view of her performance I.Q. which was in the top 2 per cent, to be scholastically much better. This scholastic underachievement may have resulted from lack of schooling or equally well from poor schooling over the last few years. In view of her intellectual capabilities and the pending 11+ decision to be made this year, she needs some particular coaching in scholastic subjects at the earliest possible convenience. Her chance of passing the 11+ at present is very low, though intellectually one would expect her to be capable of grammar-school-level work. Obviously educational coaching and some important decisions about her educational future will need to be made in the fairly immediate future. One is only surprised the situation was not noticed earlier.

Assessment: personality measurement There were no personality abnormalities in this child's profile on the Children's Personality Inventory. She emerges as a highly intelligent, mature, serious-minded and conscientious child with a certain amount of adventurousness and a liking for group activities. For her age she is a well-controlled child, though there was some degree of tenseness and anxiety.

The Child with Personality or Behaviour Problems

A fair number of children referred to the applied psychologist suffer from behaviour or personality difficulties. They may arrive in the psychology clinic because of parental or school problems via the education or medical referral systems. Until very recent years, assessment of their personalities was based on the experience and clinical acumen of the psychiatrist, paediatrician or psychologist. The recent developments in personality techniques and their sophisticated psychometric nature (described in Chapter 3) have revolutionized this situation. The value of this descriptive information on the individual child and the implications of this for psychologist, psychiatrist, paediatrician, family doctor, teacher and social worker in the treatment and handling of the child are enormous.

Case 8: difficult behaviour

Referral The seven-year-old child was the elder of a family of two children. She had become increasingly irritating and awkward to handle, extremely jealous of her younger brother, demanding attention and interest from her exasperated parents. The child had developed normally, but her school also found her aggravating and difficult. It was felt she could do her school work, but was not really trying.

Psychometric investigation In view of the inter-relations between personality difficulties, intellect and scholastic attainment, a comprehensive investigation was undertaken.

W.I.S.C.

Full scale I.Q. 104
Verbal I.Q. 100   *Performance I.Q. 107*

Verbal scales		Performance scales	
Information	13	Picture completion	11
Comprehension	9	Picture arrangement	12
Arithmetic	14	Block design	9
Similarities	8	Object assembly	10
Vocabulary	8	Coding	13
Digit span	8		

Cattell Early School Personality Questionnaire

Factor		Sten score
A	Outgoing, warmhearted	5
B	Intelligence	7
C	Emotional stability	8
D	Excitability, overactive	1
E	Dominance	8

Factor		Sten score
F	Happy-go-lucky	10
G	Super-ego strength	5
H	Socially bold	8
I	Sensitivity	6
J	Doubting, individualistic	3
N	Shrewdness	8
O	Guilt-proneness	1
Q₄	Tenseness	2

Schonell Graded Word Reading Test: R.Q. 98.

Behaviour The little girl was cooperative during the investigations and seemed to enjoy the tests.

Assessment She is of average intelligence (90–109) and there is no significant discrepancy between verbal and performance I.Q., nor is there any abnormal subtest scatter. Her R.Q. is consistent with her I.Q. level and her arithmetic score on the W.I.S.C. subtest suggests if anything that her mental arithmetic is better than might be expected for her intellectual level. Problems derived from this area would probably relate to expecting her to achieve more. She is an average child and home or school pressure to perform at grammar school level may well contribute to behaviour problems.

The Early School Personality Questionnaire gives the profile of an emotionally mature, exceptionally confident child (97 percentile point), without nervous tension. She appears extremely extraverted, interacts freely and boldly with people and is average in relation to her warmth of relationships for others.

Other factor scores are consistent with the presenting problem. She shows dominance 90 percentile point) which in this age group is aggressive, not having developed social values. Her surgency level (factor F, happy-go-lucky, enthusiastic) is as high as can be and will result in a tendency for free expression and activity as well as enthusiasm, optimism and self-confidence. Incidentally, current research suggests high surgency level is associated with a secure and affectionate family environment.

The personality pattern here is relatively clear, she is a quite stable, extraverted child with strong active and dominant tendencies. The egocentricity in her strivings will need to be firmly dealt with. In view of her stable personality and good home background, a rather *firm*, consistent, but loving programme of discipline should be started now and the situation re-assessed regularly.

Case 9: abnormal personality

Referral This is a more frequent type of the personality problem child. She had a two-year history of abdominal pain and vomiting which was aggravated by worry. At twelve years three months, she was investigated by a paediatrician. No physical reason for the abdominal pain and vomiting was found.

Psychometric investigation

W.I.S.C. (Maxwell Short Form)

Full scale I.Q. 98
Verbal I.Q. 108   *Performance I.Q. 86*

Verbal Scales		Performance scales	
Similarities	13	Block design	8
Vocabulary	10	Object assembly	7
V/P discrepancy 22			

Cattell Junior–Senior High School Personality Questionnaire

Factor		Sten score
A	Aloof – warm	2
B	Intelligence	5
C	Unstable	3
D	Phlegmatic – excitable	4
E	Submissive – dominant	5
F	Sober – enthusiastic	3

Factor		*Sten score*
G	Casual – conscientious	1
H	Timid – adventurous	2
I	Hard – sensitive	2
J	Group – individualistic	4
O	Self assured	4
Q_2	Group dependent – self sufficient	2
Q_3	Self sentiment: good – poor	4
Q_4	Relaxed – tense	4

Schonell Graded Word Reading Test: R.Q. 99.
Schonell Mechanical Arithmetic Test: Mechanical Arithmetic Quotient 90.

Assessment This girl is of average intellectual ability with a high, though not statistically significant verbal/performance discrepancy. Her scholastic attainment is also within the average range and is not inconsistent with her I.Q. Her personality, however, appears markedly abnormal. She is extremely shy, reserved and detached in her attitudes, very tough-minded, but emotionally immature and group dependent, though not particularly anxious. This child probably needs special psychological–psychiatric help and should be referred to a child psychiatric guidance unit for further investigation and treatment. The profile is not consistent with a childhood psychotic disorder.

The Clumsy Child

Professor Donald Court, Dr J. N. Walton, Dr E. Ellis and a number of other investigators in recent years have described an interesting, yet difficult group of cases known as 'clumsy children'. The problems which these children present have been related to the effect of minimal brain damage. They do not have severe paraplegias; they are not mentally defective. They may be thought of as the 'intermediate group', not brain-damaged nor severely handicapped, yet certainly not normal. Attempts to put them in the usual medical diagnostic categories of the child have failed. Perhaps psychometrics, which claims to be able to classify the child along certain dimensions of the whole, rather than to simply tag on a specific diagnostic label, will bring light on this problem and, indeed, on many others. Psychometricians are not bound by the all-or-none classification into disease groups which our medical colleagues experience.

Case 10

Referral This child was referred to our clinic at twelve years eleven months, after extensive investigation and treatment by medical and educational practitioners. His history was one of birth difficulties which suggested he might have suffered brain damage; neurologically he had certain, but not severely abnormal signs, educationally he was performing badly.

Psychometric investigation Here we have the need for extensive psychometric assessment to gain as thorough a profile analysis of this child as possible. The following measures were administered over a period of two months: W.I.S.C., Bender Gestalt, Minnesota Percepto-Diagnostic Test, Cattell High School Personality Inventory, Vineland Social Maturity Scale, Lincoln–Oseretsky Sloan edition, Schonell Diagnostic Arithmetic, English and Reading Tests.

Previous investigations Prior to the present investigation only cognitive assessments had been carried out with the W.I.S.C. Briefly, they indicated that:

W.I.S.C. (1964)

Full scale I.Q.	86
Verbal I.Q.	109
Performance I.Q.	64
V/P discrepancy	45

These had been interpreted to show that the child was educable, despite the fact that the significant V/P discrepancy suggested that the suspected brain injury had affected his intellectual capacity.

Present investigations (1966)

W.I.S.C.

Full scale I.Q. 76
Verbal I.Q. 86   *Performance I.Q. 69*
Verbal scales   *Performance scales*

Information	9	Picture completion	6
Comprehension	7	Picture arrangement	8
Arithmetic	6	Block design	8
Similarities	10	Object assembly	2
Vocabulary	7	Coding	4

V/P discrepancy   17

Bender Visual Motor Gestalt Test: Koppitz score 2 – within normal range.

Minnesota Percepto-Diagnostic Test: Raw score 51 – indication of score for emotional disturbance, borderline organic.

Lincoln–Oseretsky Motor Development Scale: Quotient less than 50 – level below that of average six-year-old.

Schonell Diagnostic Arithmetic Test: Addition quotient 52, subtraction quotient below 50, multiplication quotient below 50, division quotient below 50.

Schonell Diagnostic Reading and English Tests: Graded word reading test quotient 59, English usage quotient 55.

Cattell High School Personality Inventory

Factor		*Sten score*
A	Aloof – warm	6
B	Dull – bright	3
C	Unstable	3
D	Phlegmatic – excitable	7
E	Submissive – dominant	4
F	Sober – enthusiastic	5
G	Casual – conscientious	2
H	Timid – adventurous	3
I	Hard – sensitive	6
J	Group – individualistic	8
Q_1	Confident – insecure	7
Q_2	Group dependent – self sufficient	10
Q_3	Self sentiment: good – poor	1
Q_4	Relaxed – tense	6

Assessment Cognitively, there appears to have been a marked drop of 23 points in this child's verbal I.Q. over the two-year period since the last W.I.S.C. assessment. The performance I.Q. is still essentially the same, so his full scale level showed a drop of 10 points and the V/P discrepancy was accordingly reduced. These results are consistent with the educational assessments which show the boy to be very poor for his age in reading, English and arithmetic. His educational levels are even worse than would be expected in relation to his full scale I.Q. level (within the borderline mental defective or E.S.N. range). This is surprising even in view of the drop in verbal I.Q. and may be explained by suggesting that over the past two years he has not been benefiting from his education for other than cognitive reasons.

The personality assessment casts some light on this problem. It indicates strong neurotic traits. He was seen as a fairly timid, unstable, casual, individualistic child with general apathy and poor self regard. The Minnesota Percepto-Diagnostic Test (M.P.D.T.) was also indicative of emotional disturbance, though his social maturity score was average. These results suggest the hypothesis that his reported progressively poorer performance in class and present low educational level may have developed from personality difficulties added to his limited cognitive level. This situation is no doubt aggravated by his extremely poor Lincoln–Oseretsky Motor Development level and poor motor perceptual performance on the M.P.D.T.

As far as tests suggesting organic involvement in his difficulties are concerned, neither the W.I.S.C. V/P discrepancy nor the perceptuo-motor tests give definite organic scores, though they suggest some motor-perceptual difficulties. His motor development score is most indicative of organic lesions associated with the motor cortex areas. The motor and motor-perceptual difficulties may well be involved in his limited learning and educational attainment.

Summary and recommendations   The results show a deficiency in motor ability which is probably related to cortical damage. His present scholastic difficulties are probably due at least in part to personality problems affecting his learning ability as well as his motor-perceptual limitations. He is a very anxious boy and should benefit from treatment, possibly at a child guidance clinic, for his personality difficulties.

A special educational programme designed to take his perceptuo-motor limitations into consideration is also necessary. Further analysis of his motor and perceptual limitations is essential. The combined benefits of psychological and educational treatment are required in this case.

Summary

I have tried in this chapter to illustrate comprehensive psychometric assessment by selecting a few of the many types of problem requiring and benefiting from the application of psychometric techniques.

I hope this book proves its value in bringing the techniques and their potential to the attention of those responsible for the child in modern society. I remind readers, however, that this book has stressed diagnostic or assessment issues. Modern psychology has much to offer in the handling or treatment of the individual child and further research to develop even better assessment and treatment techniques is urgently needed. Indeed, much yet remains to be done for the individual child.

Appendix
Statistical Terms

My discussion of the psychometric assessment of the individual child necessitates the introduction of a number of statistical terms to the reader. Detailed explanation of these before would have resulted in a less clear and less readable text, with the irritation of being diverted from the main themes of the book. This glossary of terms should be useful to those not familiar with the major statistical terms employed in problems of psychological measurement.

1. The Normal Curve

The normal curve or the Gaussian distribution is a bell-shaped curve with properties intimately involved in statistical inference (see Figure 1, page 23). Mathematically, it can be described by the equation:

$$y = \frac{N}{\sigma\sqrt{(2\pi)}} e - \frac{(X - \bar{X})^2}{2\sigma^2}$$

where:

y is the height of any value
N is the number of cases
σ is the standard deviation
$\bar{X}$ is the mean of the distribution
π is 3·1416
e is 2·7183

Consequently, in a normal curve, we only need to know the mean and the standard deviation to describe it adequately. Theoretically, the curve never touches the base line, but empirically y often becomes zero.

The statistics derived from the normal curve are frequently used in psychological test construction and interpretation. The major terms used in this text are briefly explained in this appendix. For example, one may measure the I.Q.s of ten boys as:

	I.Q.			
	X	X^2	N	$= 10$
1	100	10000	ΣX	$= 1040$
2	98	9604	$(\Sigma X)^2$	$= 1081600$
3	121	14641	ΣX^2	$= 110996$
4	109	11881		
5	78	6084		
6	80	6400		
7	115	13225		
8	119	14161		
9	90	8100		
10	130	16900		

2. The Mean or Average, $\bar{X}$

The mean score $\bar{X}$ would be $\dfrac{\Sigma X}{N}$, where Σ means 'the sum of'. X is a single raw score and N is the total number of Xs or cases.

$$\bar{X} = \frac{\Sigma X}{N} = \frac{1040}{10} = 104$$

Half the sample would score above and half below this score.

3. The Standard Deviation, σ or S.D.

The standard deviation, σ, refers to the way in which scores in a normal curve spread around the mean. Three standard deviations each side of the mean account for almost the total spread of a normal curve (see Figure 1, page 23). This σ, sigma or S.D. is calculated:

$$\sigma = \sqrt{\left(\frac{\sum X^2 - \frac{(\sum X)^2}{N}}{N} \right)}$$

$$\sigma = \sqrt{\left(\frac{110996 - \frac{1081600}{10}}{10} \right)}$$

$$\sigma = 16{\cdot}9$$

4. Standard Scores, z

The standard score, z, is a statistic which denotes a transformed raw score X in terms of its deviation from a mean $\bar{X}$ in relation to the sample S.D. For any X in a distribution of scores, Xs, it can be calculated by the formula:

$$z = \frac{X - \bar{X}}{\sigma}$$

For example, the standard score, z, of boy 7 in our example would be:

$$\frac{115 - 104}{16{\cdot}9}$$

$$= 0{\cdot}65$$

As a z score is a deviation from the mean $\bar{X}$, it can be positive or negative. Boy 6's z score would be:

$$\frac{80 - 104}{16{\cdot}9}$$

$$= -1{\cdot}5$$

Furthermore, one can transform the raw scores on two measures, for example, sets of Stanford–Binet and Wechsler I.Q. scores on the same children, into z scores and compare them as a group or individually, even though the raw score Stanford–Binet and Wechsler measures are not directly comparable as their standard deviations differ. This is very convenient if a child has been tested on two or more occasions on different tests and one wishes to compare the results.

5. Percentile Point

A percentile point can also be used to place a person in relation to others on a test or compare his performance on two tests as with the z score. As the name implies, the percentile point (%ile) denotes an individual's place per 100 of the population on a given measure or test. It can be related to the percentage of people scoring at or below a certain point.

A child with an I.Q. of 115 would be on the 84th percentile, that is, 84 per cent of the population would have I.Q. equal or below that child, 16 per cent would have I.Q. above. The term may also be used to place subjects on measures of personality as in the Cattell Child and Adult Scales.

6. Correlation Coefficients

Correlation coefficients are statistics which describe the degree of relationship between any pair of measurements and are between -1 and $+1$ in extent. A correlation of $+1$ means that the two things are positively related, people obtaining a high score on one measure, say arithmetic, would obtain a high score on the other, say reading.

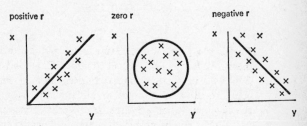

Figure 2 Diagram of positive, negative and zero correlations

Perfect $+1$ correlations are rare, but those above 0·7 may be considered high. Negative correlations (-1) describe a situation in which a high score on one variable relates to a low score on the other. For example, weight and running speed may be negatively related. A zero correlation means that there is no relationship between the two variables being measured, for example, height and intelligence.

There are several methods of calculating the correlation coefficients each applicable to certain circumstances. The most frequently used are:

The Product Moment Correlation Coefficient, r

$$r = \frac{N\Sigma XY - \Sigma X\Sigma Y}{\sqrt{[\{N\Sigma X^2 - (\Sigma X)^2\}\{N\Sigma Y^2 - (\Sigma Y)^2\}]}}$$

The Spearman–Brown Rho Coefficient, ρ

$$\rho = 1 - \frac{6\Sigma d^2}{n(n^2 - 1)}$$

7. Test Reliability

This is usually measured with reference to correlation co-efficients. In order to be predictively useful, an I.Q. or any other measurement needs to be consistent. A person measured twice on the test should obtain substantially the same score. Intelligence test scores considered reliable would usually result as positive correlations of 0·9 or more, when given on two occasions to a sample of the population. If a test is given on two occasions to a group of people and the correlation coefficient approaches zero, the measure is considered inconsistent and unreliable. One could not predict accurately from the first testing the score of an individual on the second testing. When reli-ability is presented by calculating the correlation coeffi-cient between two administrations of the test to the same individuals, it is called *test–retest reliability*. It is assumed, if the correlation is positive and high that the test accurately measures the same thing on both occasions.

The reliability of a test can also be assessed in terms of the ability of alternate items within the test to measure the same thing. This is called *split-half reliability*. For example, one may correlate scores on the odd-numbered and the even-numbered items on an intelligence test and would expect a high positive correlation.

8. Multiple Regression Equations

These equations represent or describe the contribution which a number of variables, say age and intelligence, make, or the way in which they are related to another factor, say reading level. It is basically a technical extension of the use of the degree to which things correlate. Beta, the regression coefficient, is in fact the correlation coefficient between two variables multiplied by the ratio of the standard deviations of the variables. For example, when only two variables are involved, the simple regression of intelligence on arithmetic may be described:

$$X'_1 = A + BY$$

where X' is the estimated arithmetic score for a person with Y intelligence score. A is a constant representing the difference between the mean of X and the mean of Y; B is the regression coefficient.

This allows one to predict scores on one test from actual scores on another with the highest possible accuracy. Obviously, the higher the correlation between the two measures and the closer their means and S.D.s, the more accurately one can be predicted from the other. The extension of simple regression for several factors leads to multiple regression equations. For example, one may calculate the best prediction of reading level from knowledge of a child's age, sex, intelligence, extraversion and neuroticism levels given the correct equation. The mathematics become increasingly more complicated, but not impossible, particularly with computers to ease the burden of calculation.

$$X'_1 = A + B_2X_2 + B_3X_3 + B_4X_4 + B_5X_5$$

9. The Standard Error of Estimate, S.E. est

This is a figure describing the error of measurement in a particular case. Error measurement coefficients can be calculated in relation to most statistical measures such as the mean, the S.D., and for correlations. The S.E. est discussed on page 53 refers to the multiple regression equation prediction. That is to say, the estimated arithmetic or reading scores will be plus or minus a certain amount due to error in measuring arithmetic, reading, I.Q., etc.

$$\text{S.E.est} = \sigma x \sqrt{(1 - 4x\bar{x})}$$

10. Factor Analysis

Factor analysis is an extremely sophisticated and complicated statistical technique for grouping or sorting out the correlations between variables. There are several methods of factor analysis, each of which sorts the material according to slightly different mathematical rules. They include centroid analysis, principal component analysis, several methods of rotating factors and oblique factor analysis. Basically, however, they all correlate group correlations to allow a more efficient and clearer picture of complex material to unfold. Consequently, it is frequently used to analyse complex inter-relationships. Two examples involving principal component analysis should clarify the situation. The Junior Eysenck Personality Questionnaire consists of 60 questions. When several thousand results on each item were correlated, then factor analysed, it was found that the correlations grouped in three factors each independent of the other – extraversion, neuroticism and lie scale factors. Here the factor analysis has two principal consequences. It allows the description of three personality variables to account for the children's scores on the test and gives a personality description. Secondly, the relationship or factor loading of each item to each of the factors allows the assessment of the degree to which each item contributes to extraversion, neuroticism and lie scale scores.

Factor analysis may also be used to establish the relations between a large number of measures in a precise, parsimonious manner. One may administer intelligence, personality, academic and other measures to a large number of children and obtain the intercorrelations between them. By factor analysing these correlations, we extract the main factors underlying the group of abilities or attributes measured and discussed in terms of accepted or new theoretical views about personality structure. The factors may be represented geometrically (see Figure 3). The inter-relations between the dimensions may be expressed quantitatively of course. An attempt may then be made to identify these dimensions with theoretical constructs indicating basic underlying abilities or attributes.

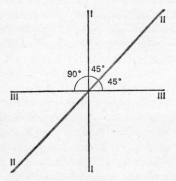

Figure 3 Diagrammatic representation of orthogonal and oblique factors

In Figure 3 factors I and II, and II and III are correlated or non-independent. Such factors are described as *oblique*.

Those on I and III are independent or uncorrelated. This situation is described as one in which the factors are *orthogonal* or at right angles to each other in geometric space – in other words, these factors are independent.

11. Analysis of Variance

Finally, analysis of variance has been mentioned earlier. This statistical technique is mathematically quite complicated. Basically, it is a series of methods which allow one to measure differences between scores or sets of scores. A simple analysis of variance would answer the question, 'Do the intelligence scores of normal, educationally retarded and educationally bright children differ significantly?'

The scores of the three groups of children, with say 100 in each group, can be analysed and compared by an F ratio calculation which states the probability level at which these groups' scores differ with respect to intelligence. If there is a 95 per cent chance that these scores represent real differences, that is, F is significant beyond the 0.5 level, the groups are considered to differ in that respect. The tests compare the variability of scores within groups, as well as the mean group scores, and can be seen to develop from the mean and S.D. concepts of statistical measurement. More complex analyses of variance designs can analyse differences between a variety of groups or factors. By comparing the appropriate variances, a single experiment can give a great deal of information. One might be interested in the effectiveness of three drugs on learning ability in three groups of patients. The learning ability score variances can be broken down into variance due to (i) group differences, (ii) drug differences and (iii) the interaction of groups and drugs, and each of these compared. In this way, one could analyse learning differences between the groups of patients, learning differences due to the action of each of the drugs, and learning differences which may occur when certain drugs were given to certain groups. It may be that one drug was more effective with one patient group, another with another, and so on.

This appendix is meant to illustrate rather than to give mathematical detail. The interested reader is referred to Harman (1960), Maxwell (1958), McNemar (1962) and Nunnally (1967) for advanced statistical and psychometric detail.

References

Anastasi, Anne (1961), *Psychological Testing*, 2nd edn, Macmillan, New York.

Bellak, L., and Sonya (1949–55), *The Children's Apperception Test 1952–55*, C.A.T. Supplement, C.P.S. and Co., New York.

Bender, L. (1938), 'Visual-motor Gestalt test and its clinical use', *American Orthopsychiatric Association Monograph*, No. 3, New York.

Benton, A. L. (1963), *The Revised Visual Retention Test*, 3rd edn, Psychological Corporation, New York.

Bill, K. R. (1958), 'An investigation into the relationship between physique, motor capacity and certain temperamental traits', *British Journal of Educational Psychology*, vol. 28, p. 2.

Brace, D. K. (1927), *Measuring Motor Ability. A Scale of Motor Ability Tests*, Baruso and Co., New York.

Burke, H. R. (1966), 'Raven's progressive matrices – a review', in Savage, R.D., *Readings in Clinical Psychology*, Pergamon Press, Oxford.

Buros, O. S. (1959 and 1965), *The Mental Measurements Yearbook*, 5th and 6th edns, Gryphen Press, New York.

Buros, O. S. (1961), *Tests in Print*, Gryphen Press, New York.

Cattell, R. B. (1959), *The Children's Personality Questionnaire*, Institute of Personality and Ability Testing, Champaign, Illinois.

Cattell, R. B. (1962), *Sixteen Personality Factor Questionnaire*, 2nd edn, Institute of Personality and Ability Testing, Illinois.

Cattell, R. B. (1963), *The High School Personality Questionnaire*, Institute of Personality and Ability Testing, Illinois.

Cattell, R. B. (1964), *The Early School Personality Questionnaire*, Institute of Personality and Ability Testing, Illinois.

Cattell, R. B. (1965), *The Scientific Analysis of Personality*, Penguin Books, Harmondsworth.

Clawson, Aileen (1962), *The Bender Visual Gestalt Test for Children*, Western Psychological Services, Los Angeles, California.

Daniels, J. C., and Diack, H. (1960), *The Standard Reading Tests*, Chatto and Windus, London.

Doll, E. A. (1947), *The Vineland Social Maturity Scale*, Education Test Bureau, Minneapolis, Minnesota.

Eysenck, H. J. (1957), *The Dynamics of Anxiety and Hysteria*, Routledge and Kegan Paul, London.

Eysenck, H. J. (1959), *The Maudsley Personality Inventory*, London University Press, London.

Eysenck, H. J. (1960), *Handbook of Abnormal Psychology*, Pitmans Medical Publications, London.

Eysenck, H. J. (1964), *The Eysenck Personality Inventory*, London University Press, London.

Eysenck, Sybil B. G. (1965), *The Junior Eysenck Personality Inventory*, London University Press, London.

Field, J. (1960), 'Two types of tables for use with Wechsler's intelligence', *Journal of Clinical Psychology*, vol. 16, pp. 3–7.

Fleishman, E. A. (1954), 'Dimensional analysis of psychomotor functions', *Journal of Experimental Psychology*, vol. 48, pp. 437–54.

Fransella, F., and Gerver, D. (1966), 'Multiple regression equations for predicting reading age from chronological age and W.I.S.C. verbal I.Q.', *British Journal of Educational Psychology*, vol. 35, pp. 86–9.

Frostig, Marianne (1967), *Testing as a Basis for Educational Therapy*, Spastic Society Conference, Oxford.

Frostig, Marianne, Lefever, D. W., Whillesley, R. D., and Maslow, Phyllis (1961–64) *Developmental Test of Visual Perception*, 3rd edn, Consulting Psychologists Press, Palo Alto, California.

Fuller, G. B. (1967), *Minnesota Percepto-Diagnostic Test*, revised edn, Psychological Corporation, New York.

Fuller, G. B., and Laird, J. T. (1963), 'The Minnesota percepto-diagnostic test', *Journal of Clinical Psychology*, vol. 19, no. 1, pp. 1–32.

Gibbins, K., and Savage, R. D. (1965), 'Study habits, personality and academic achievement', *Durham Research Review*, vol. 5, no. 16, pp. 8–12

Guilford, J. P. (1967), *The Nature of Intelligence*, McGraw Hill, New York.

Harman, H. (1960), *Modern Factor Analysis*, Chicago University Press.

Heath, S. R. (1942), 'Rail-walking performance as related to mental age and aetiological type among mentally retarded', *American Journal of Psychology*, vol. 55, pp. 240–47.

Heath, S. R. (1949), 'The rail-walking test – preliminary maturational norms for boys and girls', *Motor Skills Research*, vol. 1, pp. 34–6.

Hutt, M. L., and Briskin, G. J. (1960), *The Revised Bender Gestalt*, Grune and Stratton, New York.

Kellmer-Pringle, L. M. (1966), *Social Learning and its Measurement*, Longmans.

Klopfer, B., and Kelly, D. M. (1942), *The Rorschach Technique*, World Book Co., New York.

Koppitz, Elizabeth M. (1964), *The Bender-Gestalt Test for Young Children*, Grune and Stratton, New York.

Littell, W. M. (1966), 'The Wechsler intelligence scale for children – a review of a decade of research', in Savage, R. D., *Readings in Clinical Psychology*, Pergamon Press, Oxford.

McCarthy, J. J., and Kirk, S. A. (1961), *Illinois Test of Psycholinguistic Ability*, Institute of Research on Exceptional Children, Urbana, Illinois.

McCloy, C. H., and Young, N. (1954), *Tests and Measurements in Health and Physical Education*, 3rd edn, Appleton-Century Crofts, New York.

McNemar, Q. (1963), *Psychological Statistics*, 2nd edn, Wiley and Son, New York.

Maxwell, A. E. (1958), *Experimental Design in Psychology and the Medical Sciences*, Methuen, London.

Maxwell, A. E. (1959), 'A factor analysis of the Wechsler intelligence scale for children', *British Journal of Educational Psychology*, vol. 32, pp. 119–32.

Meehl, P. E. (1954), *Clinical vs. Statistical Prediction*, University of Minnesota, Minneapolis.

National Foundation for Educational Research (1949–61), *Mechanical Arithmetic Tests*, London.

Neale, Marie D. (1966), *Analysis of Reading Ability*, 2nd edn, Macmillan, London.

Nunnally, J. (1967), *Psychometric Methods*, McGraw Hill, New York.

Osgood, C. E. (1957), 'A behaviouristic analysis', *Contemporary Approaches to Cognition*, Harvard University Press, Cambridge, Mass.

Pascal, G. R., and Suttell, B. J. (1951), *The Bender-Gestalt Test*, Grune and Stratton, New York.

Porter, R. B., and Cattell, R. B. (1959), *Children's Personality Questionnaire*, Institute of Personality and Ability Testing, Champaign, Illinois.

Raven, J. C. (1947–53), *Guide to Using the Coloured Progressive Matrices Sets A, Ab, B*, Lewis, London.

Rorschach, H. (1921–54), *The Rorschach Psychodiagnostic Plates*, Grune and Stratton, New York.

Savage, R. D. (1965), *The Assessment of Motor Development; A Neglected Area*, Spastic Society Conference, Oxford.

Savage, R. D. (1966), *Readings in Clinical Psychology*, Pergamon Press, Oxford.

Savage, R. D., and O'Connor, D. (1966), 'The assessment of reading and arithmetic retardation in school', *British Journal of Education Psychology*, vol. 34, pp. 317–18.

Schonell, F., and Schonell, F. Eleanor (1960), *Scholastic Diagnostic and Attainment Testing*, Oliver and Boyd, London.

Sloan, W. (1955), 'Manual for the Lincoln-Oseretsy motor development scale', *Genetic Psychology Monographs*, vol. 51, pp. 185–252.

Stott, D. H. (1963), *The Social Adjustment of Children: Manual to the Bristol Social Adjustment Guides*, 2nd edn, London University Press, London.

Terman, L., and Merrill, Maud H. (1960), *A Stanford-Binet Intelligence Scale: Manual for Form L-M*, 3rd revision, Houghton Mifflin, Boston.

Tiffin, J. (1941–48), *Purdue Pegboard*, Science Research Associates, Chicago.

Tizard, J., O'Connor, N., and Crawford, J. M. (1950), 'The abilities of adolescent and high grade mental defectives', *Journal of Mental Science*, vol. 96, pp. 888–906.

Vernon, P. E. (1949), *The Grade Arithmetic – Mathematics Test*, London University Press, London.

Vernon, P. E. (1960), *Intelligence and Attainment Tests*, London University Press, London.

Vickers, Vernette, Payutz, L., and Baum, M. P. (1942), 'The brace used with young children', *Research Quarterly*, vol. 13, pp. 299–302.

Watts, A. F. (1956–60), *Sentence Reading Test I*, National Foundation for Educational Research, Newnes Educational Publishing Co., London.

Wechsler, D. (1949), *Manual for the Wechsler Intelligence Scale for Children*, Psychological Corporation, New York.

Wechsler, D. (1966), *The Wechsler Preschool and Primary Intelligence Scale*, Psychological Corporation, New York.

Yates, A. (1960), 'Abnormalities of psychomotor functions', in Eysenck, H. J., *Handbook of Abnormal Psychology*, Pitman Medical Publishing Co., London.

Index

Penguin Science of Behaviour

Penguin Modern Psychology

This series of Readings complements the *Penguin Science of Behaviour* series in providing for the student collections of papers that can be used as primary sources or as background material. The Readings are selected and introduced by leading psychologists.

Titles already available are: